NIGHT FLYER

Night Flyer

Sq. Ldr. Lewis Brandon
D.S.O., D.F.C. and Bar

NEW ENGLISH LIBRARY
TIMES MIRROR

To my wife Jean
who made it possible for me to
write this book
and
to my small daughter Felicity
who brought me cups of tea

First published in Great Britain by William Kimber Ltd., in 1961
© Lewis Brandon 1961

*

FIRST NEL PAPERBACK EDITION AUGUST 1972

*

NEL Books are published by
New English Library Limited from Barnard's Inn, Holborn, London, E.C.1.
Made and printed in Great Britain by Hunt Barnard Printing Ltd, Aylesbury, Bucks.

45001121 6

CONTENTS

Chapter I

FROM GESTAPO TO R.A.F.

I BELIEVE that I must be in a fairly good position to claim the strangest possible introduction into the Armed Forces of the Crown when I was called-up for the Royal Air Force in early January of 1941: I began my service with a week's leave and wearing the uniform of a Gestapo captain.

The explanation of this rather unlikely situation was that for some nine years before the war I had been working in British films. I had been engaged mostly in crowd work, but on occasion I had a few lines to say or a small part to play. I was in good company, for at the time Stewart Grainger, Michael Wilding, Terry Thomas and Jack Train were all likewise engaged.

I had been selected to double for Robert Donat in a scene for that delightful film *The Ghost Goes West*, which was made in 1935 by Korda's London Film Productions. I was found to resemble Donat so much that I was retained to work with the trick-camera unit on that film and later as stand-in and double on *Knight Without Armour*, in which Marlene Dietrich played opposite Donat; *The Citadel*, with Rosalind Russell as the feminine star; and finally *Goodbye Mr Chips*, with Greer Garson.

This work was most interesting, and, which was at least as important to me, it meant fairly regular work, for a stand-in was put under contract for each film. There was quite a lot to the job, for, as well as running through each scene for the benefit of the cameraman and sound department, the stand-in was often called upon to rehearse with the small-part and crowd players, so that he had to learn the dialogue and needed a fair amount of common sense and acting ability.

I was lucky enough to become quite in demand as a stand-in for one or two of the top-line cameramen, even when I hardly resembled the star at all. I worked in this capacity with Robert Newton, Michael Redgrave, Sebastian Shaw and Rex Harrison. It was while I was working on *Busman's Honeymoon,* as a stand-in for Robert Newton at Denham Studios, that I received my call-up papers for duty in the Royal Air Force.

During the pre-war years I had been one of those people who did not really believe that war would come. To me it seemed that as Herr Hitler had managed to obtain pretty well all he wanted without war, he was not likely to risk losing it all by tangling with Britain and France, two such powerful nations. When war did come, therefore, I felt very much out of it all.

I soon found that unless one had a trade, such as engineer, mechanic or carpenter, it was impossible to get into any of the Armed Forces. I had a quick bash at joining Civil Defence, but luckily the chappie who first interviewed me realised that my heart was not really in it and that I wanted something a bit more exciting. I say this without any disrespect to the men and women in Civil Defence, who did such a wonderful job, particularly during the Blitz and while the buzz-bombs were falling.

I was then in my thirtieth year. I tried vainly to volunteer for various things, including the Welsh Guards, the first regiment that I noticed were asking for non-tradesmen. All the training channels, however, were flooded with younger men who had been called-up when conscription had been introduced after Munich, a year before. I was advised to await my call-up, and eventually I was instructed to attend for a medical midway through 1940.

I was passed fit for anything and decided that the Royal Air Force appealed to me more than the other Services. Officers of the three Services were present after the medical to interview candidates and I found that I had the necessary educational qualifications for air-crew service in the Royal Air Force.

I therefore volunteered for this and had the good fortune to be accepted. I received the information, however, that it would probably be six months or so before I could expect to be actually called-up, so I carried on with my film work in the meantime.

Early in December 1941 I was working on *Busman's Honeymoon* when my call-up papers arrived. I was to report to Royal Air Force, Cardington, in a month's time and, as the film I was engaged on finished in mid-December, I found myself faced with a 'rest' that I really could not afford. I was very glad, therefore, to receive a telephone call from the Casting Department of Denham Studios to go there for a scene in Leslie Howard's film *Pimpernel Smith*.

I was to be a British naval attaché in a scene in the British Embassy in Berlin. It was only crowd work, but I was only too pleased with the prospect of taking a few extra bob into the Royal Air Force with me. At Denham I reported to the Wardrobe Department for my uniform, then to Make-up, and finally to the set, where there was the usual organised chaos that always seemed to prevail in British films.

Everyone rushed about in a leisurely manner and nothing was done that day. We all reported on the set again at nine o'clock next morning, and again not much was achieved. Halfway through the morning the Assistant Director called me and instructed me to dash up to the Wardrobe Department and change my costume for that of a Gestapo captain.

Francis Sullivan, that large and impressive actor, was playing the part of a Gestapo chief who was a guest at a ball in the British Emabassy and it had suddenly been realised that he would not attend such an important function without his aide-de-camp. Nobody had been cast for this part, so I had been roped in.

As a precautionary measure, I pointed out to the Assistant Director that I was due to report to Cardington in ten days' time, but he assured me that the Embassy set was to be demolished in four days' time to make way for another set and that the scene had been scheduled for only three days' shooting. There should be no difficulties, therefore.

Francis Sullivan and I had to arrive as guests at the Embassy, where we had reason to believe that we would find the Pimpernel, who had been helping enemies of the State to escape. There was a scene in an ante-room, where we expected to find a vital clue in an invitation card with the Pimpernel's name on it and with a piece missing. Imagine our disgust when we found that nearly all the invitation cards had the identical piece missing.

We were then introduced to the Ambassador and made our way down a vast staircase, where we had a perfect opportunity of observing most of the assembled guests. I had to point to a bearded character standing by a large fireplace and mutter:

'What about that fellow over there with the beard?'

Sullivan snubbed me with the retort: 'Don't be a fool, he is one of our men!'

It may well be thought that three days would be more than ample time for filming a sequence of this sort, but it was not so. The days went merrily by until I had only three days before reporting to Cardington. Although I am not a worrying type, I began to wonder what would happen. The film unit must finish the sequence with me or have to re-shoot the entire scene with someone else – a most expensive business.

I had a word with the assistant director, who had a chat with the director, who had a chat with the production manager, who assured everyone that all would be well: the set was to be pulled down next day and I would have a couple of days to myself before my call-up.

It was not to be. We did not finish that day, and after the next day's shooting it became obvious even to the production manager that I would be required for several more days. He therefore phoned the Adjutant at Cardington, used the magic word 'Films' and I was given a week's leave from the R.A.F. before I had even joined it – to play a Gestapo officer, too!

10

The scene was eventually finished and I did manage to have a couple of days to myself before reporting to Cardington, where the Adjutant obviously thought I must be a pretty well-known actor and wanted to hear of some of my more important parts.

I spent ten days at Cardington, where I was issued with my uniform and the rest of my kit. I was to wear the uniform for the next fourteen years, although I had no suspicion of this at the time. I had various inoculations and learnt that a body of men must always march from one place to another.

Bridgnorth was my next posting for three weeks' square bashing, then, as there was a bottleneck in air-crew training, I was posted to Acklington, in Northumberland, where I had to await my turn to go to an Initial Training Wing. There my idea of life in the R.A.F., which had been fairly comfortable at Cardington and Bridgnorth, took a distinct downward plunge.

Our billets had to be seen to be believed. We were in a barn above an inhabited cowshed, about forty of us, with one cold-water tap as the only piece of modern plumbing available for all our needs. It was February, bitterly cold, with plenty of snow around. The station had, in fact, only recently regained contact with the outside world after having been cut off by snow for several days. We of the cowshed were classified as aircraft hands/general duties, an involved way of saying that we were spare bods and could be used for any duty. These palatial billets were a couple of miles away from the camp and the journey was made in a lorry which usually stopped a hundred yards or so from the cowshed, hooted and then made off before any of us could get near enough to climb aboard.

The good fortune that I was to experience for nearly all my Service life started fairly early. Probably because of my height, nearly six feet two inches, I was sorted out to help in the guard-room as a Service policeman. This meant transferring to billets on the station and made life a great deal more comfortable than it had been in the cowshed.

Acklington was then a very important day-fighter station,

with two Spitfire squadrons responsible for the defence of much of the north-east coast. My duties as a Service policeman involved me in a fair amount of walking around the airfield and the surrounding area. Whilst I was ambling about I noticed a dozen or more wooden poles in various places around the airfield. These poles were arranged so that they pointed up into the air at an angle of about forty-five degrees and were painted to look like camouflaged anti-aircraft guns. The country was so short of light ack-ack guns that few, if any, could be spared even for an important airfield such as Acklington. The only weapons most of the airmen carried were chunks of metal fencing – known as pikes. This was quite an insight into our state of preparedness for war. I did not see much change in these conditions in the three months I was at Acklington, but luckily the Hun must have been too busy elsewhere to attack us.

The next move for me was to the Aircrew Receiving Wing at Stratford-on-Avon, where I spent an extremely pleasant three weeks. I had never been in that part of the world before and found it really delightful, perhaps all the more so because there were no tourists and sightseers to spoil things.

One day I was in a canoe on the Avon when a punt suddenly shot out from the bank and my strenuous efforts to avoid it caused the canoe to overturn, shooting me, in full uniform, into a very cold river. The wartime airman's uniform was so shapeless that it looked no different from normal when it was saturated so that I walked back to my billets without anyone noticing.

The Air Crew Selection Board at Stratford decided that I was too old for training as a pilot and too bulky to fit into the small turret that air gunners used. The only job left was that of navigator; I did not mind particularly, but I had no choice, anyhow.

I was posted to an Initial Training Wing at Scarborough for an eight-week course. Pilots and navigators made up the course in about equal numbers, and after five weeks the pilots-to-be were suddenly required at an Elementary Flying Training School. Off they went, and the navigators were put to filling sandbags for the last three weeks of the course – a very agreeable occupation on the beach at Scarborough in early June, with the weather just about as nice as it could be.

One Sunday morning our sandbagging was interrupted by a summons to report back to our hotels immediately. Almost all the hotels had, of course, been taken over by the R.A.F., so that we were living in comfort.

Back at our hotel we were addressed by the Commanding Officer, who asked if any of us would like to volunteer for flying duties on night fighters. The C.O. could tell us very little about the job, but the main points that appealed to me were three in number: it meant a shorter course than the normal navigation course; the pay would be the same; and the volunteers would have to go the Air Ministry in London for an interview. As I was a Londoner, I did not hesitate at all but decided to try it.

The job of a straight navigator apparently called for fairly good ability at maths and that had never been a particularly good subject of mine, even when I had been at school some fifteen years before; I had been looking forward to my navigation course with a deal of trepidation. We had spent most of the first five weeks at Scarborough marching, drilling and learning elementary navigation, with a little maths revision thrown in for good measure. I had been getting rather worried about the maths, which seemed no easier after the passage of years, so that this call for night fighters came at a perfect time for me.

I was one of some two dozen who set off from our Wing for the interview in the Big City. From the very beginning everything to do with the night-fighting business was wrapped in mystery. We were instructed before our interviews began that we were not to discuss what took place during the interviews with anyone when we returned to our units. I remember being shown several diagrams and designs and having to assess relative sizes without having the slightest idea what it was all about, and I certainly could not tell from my interrogator's expression if my answers were the ones required. Anyhow, I enjoyed my forty-eight hours in London, and a few days after my return to Scarborough I was informed that, with half a dozen other chaps from my Wing, I had been selected for training as a night-fighter navigator.

The training was to be carried out at Prestwick, near Ayr, where Number Three Radio School was situated. I found to my delight that the course was only three weeks, compared with the three or four months of the normal navigation course. Just a small corner of the veil of mystery that always shrouded the hush-hush job of night fighting was lifted for us at Prestwick. We were to be instructed in the use of 'A.I.' These letters stood for 'Airborne Interceptor', a magical piece of equipment devised by the 'Boffins' to aid night fighters in their tsak of seeking out the enemy in the dark. The brains that had conceived the early-warning radar system that had been such an essential factor during the Battle of Britian had now produced a radar set small enough to be carried in an aircraft and which could detect the presence of another aircraft. This information was presented to the navigator of a night-fighter crew in such a way that by the use of a little common sense he should be able to chase and intercept an enemy aircraft in the dark. I was to be one of the very first batch of aircrew under training to be instructed in the use of this apparatus.

I was now brought up to date with developments in the air war in general and the night war in particular so that I could appreciate the situation as it was then in July 1941.

The German Air Force was known as the *Luftwaffe*, the literal translation for which is 'Air Weapon.' Its original purpose was to act as a sort of super long-range artillery for the German armies, a spearhead for the *Blitzkrieg*. It was intended to operate almost exclusively by day, and very little time, if any, had been devoted to night flying, a state of affairs that was to have severe repercussions for the Germans later.

The responsibility for the defence of Great Britain from air attack fell upon Fighter Command, who began the war with inadequate resources, both in men and machines. Fortunately this inadequacy was offset to a large extent by a long-range warning system of radar stations, sited at strategic points round the coast and capable not only of detecting aircraft flying at medium height, say eight thousand feet, a hundred miles away, but also of enabling their movements to be plotted. This meant that instead of a few fighters having to maintain standing patrols all day long, they could be at readiness on the ground. When a suspect plot was seen on the radar, our fighters could be sent off to intercept the incoming raid, with their petrol tanks full and the pilots fairly well rested.

For purposes of control of our fighters the country had been split up into four areas. Number 10 Group operated south and west of Oxford; Number 11 Group from the south coast to a line running east and west through Bedford; Number 12 Group from this line to a similar line through York; and 13 Group north of that.

The Groups were subdivided into Sectors, each of which contained a number of fighter stations, one of which was selected as Sector Station, with its own operations-room in which the Sector Controller could watch the movements of raids in his area and have radio control of his fighters.

The Fighter Command operations-room was used mainly for organising reinforcement from one Group to another, if this became necessary, while the Group operations-rooms, with a broader picture than the Sectors, allocated the squadrons to counter a particular raid.

This system worked well against the daylight raids of the Battle of Britain in 1940. From the long range warning radar information came in giving the news of the approach of an enemy force, its approximate size and the route it was taking. The defending squadrons were scrambled, told the course to steer to enable them to intercept the raid as far out to sea as possible and then given any further information which might help them. Once the fighters saw their quarry, the cry of 'Tally-ho' came over the radio and the battle was on.

The Sector Controller could, if necessary, bring his fighters to within about five miles of the enemy; in fact, however, the fighters would almost always see them before then. Bombers attacking in daylight usually had an escort of fighters to protect them and would also fly in formation so as to give each indivi-

15

dual bomber the benefit of the protection of as many guns as possible. The job of our day fighters was to separate the enemy fighters from the bombers, shoot down as many bombers as possible and break up the bomber formations.

At night fighters were dealt with as individual aircraft and Sector had complete control over them.

As night bombers attacked under cover of darkness, they were able to dispense with fighter escort. Then, too, because of protection afforded by darkness, they did not have to rely on the concentrated fire power of a formation for their defence. These things, added to the obvious difficulties of formation flying for long periods at night, meant that each bomber must be regarded as a separate menace by our controllers, so that a night bomber raid meant a series of individual interceptions, one fighter after one bomber.

We in this country were not subjected to mass raids, when bombers operated in hundreds all dropping their bombs within a short space of time, so that the individual interception remained the best method of dealing with the night bomber over Britain. Nevertheless, there were many difficulties to be overcome before night fighters could operate with much chance of success.

The early night fighters had lots of troubles to contend with. Their radio communication with the ground was very indistinct and had only a short range. Although they had to fly in the dark, the instruments provided for the pilot and on which he relied for blind-flying were poor. The airfields from which they flew had inadequate airfield lighting, and few airfields had decent runways. If the pilots overcame all these difficulties, even then they were not likely to achieve much more than an ineffectual chase around the night skies and then have to find the way home, without an effective homing device.

The Sector Controller could bring the night fighter to within five miles or so of a target, which was enough in daylight, but, even in clear conditions, at night the fighter would not see an enemy aircraft until he was about 1,200 feet away, even if he knew exactly where to look. When the Sector Controller had done all that he could, the only further help was afforded by searchlights. The searchlights were being operated with sound detectors, however, so that by the time the plots were worked out and used the bomber had probably travelled quite a distance and, because of this inherent time lag, the searchlight usually trailed some way behind the bomber and was quite likely to illuminate the stalking fighter instead.

Still, the searchlights did sometimes catch a bomber in their beams and any lucky fighter who happened to be near enough could make for the cone of lights. A few German bombers were shot down by this means and anything that brought results was a help.

So far as anti-aircraft guns were concerned, a separate Anti-Aircraft Command had been formed early in 1939 and had been placed under the direction of Fighter Command. Their detection equipment, however, was similar to that used by the searchlights, and until they received better means of laying their guns they were effective only as a deterrent, forcing the bombers to fly higher and thus making accurate bombing more difficult.

The powers-that-be were only too well aware of these short-comings and of our vulnerability to night bombers. Every effort was made during the first year of the war to put things right, with the most remarkable success, as I hope to show later. In the meantime the most desperate measures were resorted to or discussed, even if they had only the remotest possibility of success.

Such unlikely schemes were considered as that some of our aircraft should fly at right angles to the enemy's course and above them, trailing long lengths of piano wire in the hope that the wires would become entangled in the enemy's propellers. Or, it was suggested some of our heavy aircraft should fly above and ahead of the raiders, dropping out small aerial mines on parachutes for the bombers to collide with, or magnesium flares on parachutes to illuminate the bombers and enable our fighters to dive in and shoot them down.

Most of these schemes and many more were tried out, although, with the possible exception of the last idea, the chances of success were small indeed.

The job of night fighting and day fighting in bad weather when single-seater single-engined fighters could not operate, had originally been given to Blenheim squadrons. The Bristol Blenheim was a twin-engined aircraft that had been designed as a medium bomber. It had a single machine-gun in a turret operated by an air gunner, and four machine-guns were added to the fighter version. These four guns were bolted to the fuselage of the aircraft and were under the control of the pilot, so that he had to aim his aircraft at the target in order to shoot at it. The Boulton Paul Defiant, a single-engined fighter with a similar crew of pilot and air gunner, later joined in the almost hopeless task of hunting the enemy bombers by night.

The very few successes gained by these early night fighters were, perforce, achieved in conditions of bright moonlight. It did not take the wily Hun very long to become aware of this fact and to avoid coming over in conditions of that sort.

Another difficulty that arose was that of positive identification at night. Before opening fire, the night fighter had to recognise the target as hostile. This meant getting in very close, with the attendant risk of being spotted by the bomber who would take violent evasive action before the fighter could aim his guns and would probably escape.

It was important, too, that the night fighter should have sufficient fire power to ensure that if he did get an enemy bomber in his sights he should be able to blow it out of the sky first go, or at least damage it so severely that it would be badly handicapped in taking evasive action.

No absolutely reliable and positive means of identification of friend or foe was in fact produced during the last war. On defensive night fighting visual identification always had to be made, whilst even on offensive operations over enemy territory the only exception to this rule was if an aircraft was seen taking off from or attempting to land on an enemy airfield.

Although some fairly efficient means of identification of friend or foe were produced, it will be seen that the fact that a target was not displaying 'identification friend or foe' could not be taken as positive proof that it was hostile. The target might be a friend whose I.F.F. was not working or not switched on. In other words, I.F.F. could give positive proof that a target was friendly, and thus save an unnecessary chase, but it could not be assumed that no I.F.F. meant that the target was definitely hostile.

These varied and intricate problems were being tackled by the best brains available during 1939 and 1940. One by one the difficulties were overcome. A new very-high-frequency radio telephony apparatus had been developed with far greater clarity and range than the old radio. Blind flying instruments had been vastly improved and better airfield lighting with good runways had been installed at night fighter bases. A.I., the airborne interception apparatus whose secrets were to be revealed to me at Prestwick, had been thought of as far back as 1936.

Seemingly endless problems had been resolved, and in 1939 and 1940 early marks of A.I. had been used in Blenheims, with great promise of things to come. A new night-fighter aircraft, the Bristol Beaufighter, started coming into squadron service late in 1940. This aircraft had been fitted with V.H.F. radio, A.I., reasonably reliable blind-flying instruments, and was armed with four 20-mm. cannons and six .303 machine-guns. This truly formidable armament was all controlled by the pilot, who had to aim the Beaufighter at the target and who fired the whole broadside by pressing a button.

The answers had been found to most of the night fighters' problems, but, unfortunately, not in time for the Blitz of 1940, when the German bombers had been so ineffectually opposed.

Fighter Command was very much a pilots' command, as one would expect, with the result that when the boffins put the magic black boxes of A.I. in the Blenheims little thought had been given to the chap who had to operate the set. It took Command some time to wake up to the idea that the equipment really worked and that it was temperamental. It needed a fairly intelligent member of aircrew to get the best out of it, and pilot and operator must be able to work together as a team.

It was decided, therefore, to select aircrew specifically for this job and I had been lucky enough to be awaiting training at the Initial Training Wing at Scarborough just when the very first selection had been made.

I found at Prestwick that there was a very good reason for the short three-week course. So few people had any first-hand knowledge of its operational working that all we could be shown in any detail was the theoretical use of the set and of the control knobs with which it fairly bristled. In the classroom A.I. sets had been arranged on benches so that we could become accustomed to the controls, the most important of which were the tuning and volume, or gain controls. An ingenious piece of apparatus, a synthetic trainer, had been devised to give us a rough idea of what we might expect to see in the air, and there were a few A.I. equipped Blenheims in which we could eventually see for ourselves what the whole business was about.

Our instructor explained to us that A.I. worked on exactly the same principle as a sound echo. If you shout into a cave, or across a valley, the sound waves from your voice hit the far side and are reflected back to you. The night fighter carrying A.I. transmitted a series of radio waves, and if they hit anything they would be returned to the fighter as an echo.

Just as the width of the valley could be calculated from the time the echo took to travel back, so could the range of the object hit by the transmitter's waves be estimated. On this was based the whole conception of A.I.

There were three vital pieces of information that a night fighter must have in order to chase an enemy at night: how far away the target was, whether it was above or below the fighter, and where it was in relation to the fighter in the horizontal plane – port or starboard. A.I. could provide all this information.

The transmitter was in the nose of the aircraft and the transmitting aerial looked like a large arrowhead with two barbs. The front barb was the actual aerial whilst the second barb was a reflector which helped to concentrate maximum power forward, as the fighter was most concerned with chasing something in front of him.

To pick up the echo, there were four receiving aerials arranged in two pairs. The first pair were mounted on either wing tip for the horizontal or azimuth plane; the second pair were placed one on the upper surface of a wing and the other on the lower surface for the vertical or elevation plane. The idea behind this positioning of the aerials was that a target above and to starboard would be picked up more strongly by the aerials on the upper-wing surface and on the starboard wing tip than by the other two aerials. The extra strength in the signals received by these two aerials could be measured and would then give the information required.

The information was presented to the operator on two cathode ray tubes: the azimuth tube indicated the signals received by the wing-tip aerials, and the elevation tube showed the signals from the upper- and lower-wing surface aerials. These tubes were the business end of A.I.

The synthetic trainer on which we were shown what we might expect to see in the air had two cathode ray tubes in a frame which we learnt was known as the indicator unit. It is simpler to consider these one at a time. The Azimuth tube gives range and bearing of the target from the fighter. Running through the centre of the tube there was a luminous green line known as the time trace. Attached to the time trace and covering almost a third of the tube we saw a triangle of light that looked like a Christmas tree etched in green light. The triangular shape was formed by the ground echo or ground return; just as an aircraft would send back an echo, so did the ground, though the echo from the ground was of course very much stronger than that from an aircraft.

The lower the fighter aircraft was flying, the further down the tube the ground return would come – the Christmas-tree stem would grow short, and the foliage would spread over more of the tube – so that eventually, when the fighter was down to about 600 feet in height, it would cover the entire tube and blot out any other echoes. Thus the performance of A.I. depended largely on the height above the ground at which the fighter could fly. This snag was overcome to a large extent in later marks of A.I., but in Mark 4 A.I., which was in use at this time, it was something that had to be accepted.

An aircraft echo appeared in the shape of a diamond, sitting astride the time base line – the stem of the Christmas-tree. The distance of this diamond or 'blip' from the root end of the Christmas-tree stem indicated the range of the target from the fighter. The position of the blips on the time base line showed if the target was dead ahead or to one side. The blip always remained astride the time base line, but could move over towards one side or the other as the target altered course.

The elevation tube worked on exactly the same principle, but had been turned over on its side for easier interpretation. A target that was above the fighter would produce a blip on the elevation tube with most of the diamond above the time base. By constantly watching the movements of the blips on the two tubes the operator could, after much practice, assess not only the position of the target but which way it was moving. By a series of orders to his pilot he could then intercept.

This, then, was what we were to be trained for.

I see from my flying log book that I flew four times in the Blenheims at Prestwick. I had absolutely no flying experience at all prior to this, so I should have been very impressed. In fact I was not. The Blenheims had been adapted for use as flying classrooms so that an instructor with a couple of pupils could huddle together in a small, blacked-out compartment and gaze at the little green etchings on the cathode ray tubes. It was most important that the clearest possible picture should be obtained and frequent adjustments had to be made to the tuning control, the gain control and various other knobs that affected the brightness and clarity of the picture. It was rather like fiddling with an early television set. Soon after the aircraft took off, the A.I. would be switched on and the adjustments made. This was known as 'setting-up', and proved a great deal more difficult in an aeroplane than on the ground sets.

ELEVATION TUBE   AZIMUTH TUBE

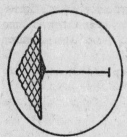

Fighter flying at 14,000 feet height. Target blip just emerging from Ground Returns. Target range about three miles, showing above and to starboard. (These diagrams give a simplified picture and make no allowances for the various forms of interference.)

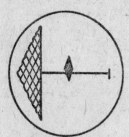

Range of target has now decreased to just under two miles. Showing about fifteen degrees above and twenty degrees starboard.

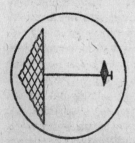

Range of target is now approaching minimum range; it is about 1,000 feet away, showing about ten degrees above and ten degrees starboard. At this stage a visual by the pilot should be imminent.

The Blenheims took off in pairs so that each could in turn provide a target for the other and enable the learner operators to see what a blip looked like in the air. Each pupil would have a go at setting up the picture and then try to interpret to the instructor what the target aircraft was doing. The instructor would then turn some of the knobs to upset the picture and the next pupil would have to set it up again and then interpret what he saw.

The Blenheims would then change over; the one that had been acting as fighter would become target and the same procedure would take place. The pupils in the target aircraft practised setting up and were also able to practise using a very important device that had been incorporated in A.I.

By turning a switch the set could be used for a completely different purpose. The transmitter in the aircraft triggered off a beacon situated at the aircraft's home base. The response of the beacon could be picked up on the azimuth aerials of the aircraft and the navigator would thus be able to read off the aircraft's bearing and distance from base. This was the homing device that night fighters had needed so badly. It proved to be one of the simplest and most reliable navigation aids ever produced. The signal from the ground beacon could be coded to flash a Morse letter combination on to the A.I. in the aircraft, and each night fighter station had its own coded beacon.

Operators carried a map of Britain with these night stations marked on it and with the code letters of each station shown. Wherever one flew over Britain, it was always possible to pick up two or more of these beacons, so that there was no excuse for getting lost as long as the A.I. was working.

My total flying time at Prestwick was five and a half hours. During this time I had not had time to feel air-sick; we had been kept so busy and I had really had no opportunity of deciding whether or not I liked flying. We had clambered into the darkened interior of the Blenheims, all cluttered up with flying clobber and unable to see out at all. A door had been shut tight and we would hear the thunder of the engines starting up.

A bumping motion would denote that we were taxying around the perimeter track, and an extra loud burst of sound from the engines and the cessation of the bumps would mean that we were airborne. At the end of the flight the pilot would tell us to hang on tight, as we were about to land; there would be a large bump, followed by a few smaller bounces and we would know we had landed.

Chapter II

NIGHT-FIGHTER SQUADRON

I HAD thought myself extremely lucky to be on the course at Prestwick and my luck was to hold. At nearby Heathfield Number 141 Squadron were engaged in re-equipping with Beaufighters. They had been a Defiant squadron, with air gunners and pilots, some of whom did not relish the change to Beaus. It was quite understandable; air gunnery was the trade for which these chaps had trained and many of them wished to retain their trade. A few of the pilots preferred flying the single-engined Defiant to the twin-engined Beau, and with the gunners who did not wish to become A.I. operators they were to be transferred to another Defiant squadron.

Number 141 Squadron therefore urgently needed some bods to replace the gunners and obtained permission from the Air Ministry to take half a dozen pupils from Prestwick. I was one of the lucky ones. Instead of a further course at an Operational Training Unit, I found myself posted to Heathfield as a sergeant on probation. To be on an operational squadron after only a three-week course seemed just too good to be true.

With the five other chaps who had been selected from Prestwick I found myself a fledgling in the sergeants' mess. For a short time we were looked upon as jumped-up young sprogs, but soon we all fitted in well enough. It was unnatural that these N.C.O.s, many of whom had been slogging away for years to reach their rank, should be a trifle envious and resentful that we had earned our sergeant's stripes so easily.

I found that the normal set-up on a night-fighter squadron consisted of two flights, 'A' Flight and 'B' Flight. Each of these was commanded by a Squadron Leader, while the Squadron Commander carried the rank of Wing Commander. The Commanding Officer of 141 Squadron was Wing Commander G. F. W. Heycock, who was referred to as the C.O., the 'Old Man' or simply as 'Heykers'.

I joined 141 Squadron on August 1st, 1941, and for the first few days I busied myself in learning something of the layout of Heathfield, squadron organisation and mess life. I was allocated to 'B' Flight, which had its own dispersed site.

One of the lessons that had been learned during the Battle of Britain was the necessity to disperse aircraft and their crews so that a single attack by enemy bombers could not write off the operational potential of an airfield. Aircrews had to be within easy reach of their aircraft, so huts were built at dispersed sites around the airfield. Permanent sleeping quarters and messes were also spread around as much as possible.

On night-fighter stations this entailed the building of dispersal huts complete with cooking and sleeping facilities in order to avoid the constant use of transport at all hours of the night. The night-fighter dispersal huts were rather like exclusive little clubs. They were made as comfortable as possible and crews awaiting their turn to fly amused themselves with conversation, chess and cards, or perhaps just dozed. Every ear however, would be attuned to listen for the ring of the operations' telephone, which might ring at any moment to order off aircraft if there was any enemy activity. On most squadrons, all aircrew, officers and N.C.O.s, shared all the facilities equally, but one or two squadrons ran things rather on a Gentlemen and Players' basis – fortunately, I was never to be on one of these squadrons.

Number 141 Squadron had been engaged in the Battle of Britain flying Defiants, an aircraft that was really a compromise between a day fighter and a night fighter. It was a single-engined two-seater aircraft whose four machine-guns were in a power-operated turret just behind the pilot and controlled by an air gunner. With its unconventional armament, the Defiant had some considerable successes at first against German day fighters and bombers, but once the enemy cottoned on to its armament the Defiant was no match for their day fighters, and was relegated to the night role.

Number 141 Squadron had been night-fighting for almost a year when they were re-equipped with Beaufighters. The re-equipment had only just begun when I joined them, so that the Bristol Beaufighter was just as new to the older members of the squadron as it was to me. There were six or seven Beaus already on the squadron, and they were in constant use as the pilots strove to obtain enough experience on them to be declared operational.

A couple of lectures were laid on to give them some idea of what A.I. could do, for it was something quite new to them. Nearly all the pilots had been chasing about in the dark, without much success, for a year or so. Although they hoped that this A.I. stuff might be of some use, I could well understand that many of them were only prepared to take it with a pinch of salt; they had seen so many of these bright ideas come to naught. Besides, most of them had desperately wanted to be on day fighters, which seemed to offer a great deal more action, so that they were rather disgusted with the night lark.

During the afternoon of August 6th I had my first trip in a Beau, flying as operator for one of the officers whose air gunner had gone to Prestwick for a quick A.I. course. We were up for an hour and spent nearly all the time trying out the homing device of the A.I. I found that I could pick up the Heathfield beacon very easily and had no difficulty in bringing the Beau back to the airfield several times. All I had to do was to identify the beacon on my A.I. set, tell the pilot to turn until the blip was sitting nicely astride the time base and read off the distance as we approached. I could tell that the pilot was quite impressed; as we walked back to dispersal he said: 'Well, at least part of the ruddy stuff works!'

For my part, I was most impressed with my first real flight and with my introduction to the Beau. Although I had flown in the Blenheims at Prestwick, I had not been able to see what was going on, whereas in the Beau I had a grandstand view. It struck me that I was going to like this flying business.

The Beaufighter was quite an impressive aircraft. It had a tough, bulldog look about it with its snub nose and powerful twin Hercules engines. The two main landing wheels of the undercarriage were housed in the engine nacelles when in flight, and there was a small rear wheel which did not retract. Under the nose were four canvas patches which covered the gunports for the Hispano cannons and six similar patches on the leading edge of the wings covered the nozzles of the machine-guns. The Beau certainly packed a punch.

A hatch opened downward from the belly of the Beau and the crew got in through this; it led into a small well behind the pilot's cockpit. The cockpit itself seemed filled with dials and knobs and was quite roomy. In front of the pilot was a large expanse of bullet-proof windscreen, giving pretty good all-round visibility. In the centre of the cockpit was a massive control column and on that was a button with which the pilot could fire all the guns simultaneously.

Behind the pilot's compartment were two armour-plated doors through which was the A.I. department. The floor consisted of a fairly wide cat-walk, on either side of which were the breech blocks and mechanisms of the four cannons. On racks attached to the sides of the fuselage were racks to hold drums of cannon shells, each drum weighing about sixty pounds and holding sixty shells. A drum was fitted to each cannon before taking off, and had to be replaced with a fresh one if a combat took place, and reloading became necessary. The drums were rather unwieldy and difficult to fit correctly while the aircraft was in flight, but fortunately they were soon to be replaced with a belt-feed system that required no attention during flight.

There was a Perspex dome about halfway along the fuselage and under it was a swivel seat for the A.I. operator. The A.I. set was fitted behind the seat so that the way forward should not be impeded at all if the cannon needed attention. The operator was therefore facing backwards when operating his set but could swivel round in his seat if he wished to see what was going on ahead.

It was realised that night fighting with the new equipment would essentially be a matter of team work between pilot and operator so that the teaming up of a crew was of considerable importance. A couple of days after my Beau flight I was crewed with 'Lofty' Hamer, a very experienced Flight Sergeant. Straight away he told me to get into a Defiant, the only aircraft that was available, and off we went for a little local flying.

I found that I could just squeeze into the turret of the Defiant – it had not been designed for a fourteen-stone six-footer. By keeping my elbows close to my sides and crouching down in the seat I just fitted in. Once we were off the ground I gingerly moved the control that swung the turret round and found to my relief that I did not get caught up on anything.

Presumably Lofty Hamer was wondering what sort of sprog he had been crewed with. He certainly wasted no time in finding out. That Defiant began to do things that I had only dimly realised were possible in an aircraft; things I had never even seen from the ground. Now I was in an aircraft actually doing them: rolls and a loop or two; steep turns and a power dive – the lot. Then we were flying straight and level over the sea and I had come through my test. At least Lofty knew I would not be troubled with air-sickness on any future flight.

I had noticed that in the Defiant I had great difficulty in understanding what was being said on the R/T, which was very indistinct indeed. In comparison, the Beau's R/T had been crystal clear, for it was fitted with the new V.H.F. radio. There was also a separate intercom system between pilot and operator in the Beau which cut out all other sounds and was very clear indeed.

As Heathfield was near the west coast of Scotland it was by no means a highly operational station, but it was an ideal station for a squadron to re-equip. We could get to know our box of tricks with all its vagaries, while the pilots could familiarise themselves with the flying characteristics of the Beau. Although as a squadron we were occasionally called on for an operational patrol, nobody had a chase after an enemy aircraft during the five and a half months we were there.

I am convinced that it was this thorough grounding and long practice period that led to future successes. I found, too, that in these early days the quick and reliable homings that we were able to give our pilots helped tremendously in giving them confidence in the capabilities of A.I.

They soon found that we could give them an immediate and reliable distance and bearing from base when we were using the beacon range. When we switched over to interception range, unless the operator was quite clueless, it was not long before the pilot was convinced that that part of the A.I. could work equally well. It all required lots and lots of practice on the part of both pilot and operator, however, and the spell at Heathfield gave us the opportunity for this practice.

A few days after joining 141 Squadron I reached my thirtieth birthday. I was one of the oldest members of the squadron and I found then and later that the fact that I was considerable junior in rank to men much younger than I was tended to make me feel as if I was still in my teens. Perhaps I had hit upon the secret of eternal youth!

After my initiation into real flying with Lofty Hamer I found it thrilling and absorbing. The constant challenge to master the A.I. soon made me realise that I had been fortunate enough to fall into what was probably one of the most interesting and exciting jobs in any of the Services.

Although we were seldom called on for operational patrols, the squadron settled down to routine. The two flights each did two nights on duty followed by two nights off. The flight starting its two days on duty would assemble at dispersal soon after breakfast; the serviceability of the aircraft would be ascertained and crews would be allotted to fly in those that were ready.

Each flight had a complement of eight aircraft plus two reserves and usually twelve complete crews so as to allow for leave or sickness. The remainder of the Beaus were not long in arriving and our re-equipment was soon completed, so that full-scale training could go on apace.

To ensure that the maximum amount of practice was obtained from every precious hour of flying, the Beaus always took off in pairs, just as the Blenheims had at Prestwick. Each would take a turn as fighter and then as target. We were flying mostly in daylight at first until the pilots gained enough experience in flying the Beaus to be able to take off and land in the dark. This meant that all the time the operator was interpreting what he could see on his A.I. the pilot could actually see the target aircraft visually, so that he was in a good position to judge for himself the reliability of the set and the ability of his operator.

A series of flying exercises had been worked out so that the fighter would approach the target at varying angles. At first the operator just read off to his pilot what he could see on his tubes. One exercise was entirely confined to practice on the elevation tube; that is to say, the target would be either well above or well below and the operator had to constantly tell the pilot how his height variation was changing. The operator could tell the range of the target from either the azimuth or elevation tube, and it was the range of the target from the fighter that was of most interest and importance to the pilot. The more frequently he was given the range of a target in the dark, the easier it would be for him to ensure that he was not overtaking it too fast. Then, too, knowing that on most nights he should see a target at about 1,500 feet, he would be prepared for the visual sighting.

After the initial exercises had been carried out to the satisfaction of the pilot, the operator began to practise interceptions. Instead of just telling the pilot what he could see, he had to give instructions to the pilot so that the fighter aircraft turned after the target at the appropriate moment, chased it and, ideally, finished up just behind, slightly below and at about the same speed as the target.

The theory of the art of night interception was based on

facts that had been learnt the hard way by the Defiant and Blenheim crews. If a fighter was approaching a bomber on a converging course and the fighter turned after it too soon, he might well finish up in front of the bomber. Too late a turn would result in a long chase from astern, with consequent waste of time and the probability that the bomber might be given sufficient time to drop his bombs on target and scoot for home.

Careful speed control on the part of the fighter was important if the pilot was to be able to spot the bomber, identify it and then bring his guns to bear on it, if possible without being seen. On most nights, the position from which the night-fighter pilot would be best placed to get a visual on the bomber was from slightly below and almost dead astern. On an average dark night the range at which he could expect to see the bomber was between 1,000 and 1,500 feet. On a very dark night, without benefit of starlight, he might have to close in to 600 or 800 feet before the vital visual. He would be searching for the vague silhouette of the bomber in the darkness, but he had two important things to help him. His operator would tell him just where to look for the bomber and, if approaching from slightly below astern, he might see the exhaust flames from the bomber's engines.

On any night there was always one section of the sky that was just a little lighter than the rest. Once the interception was well under way and the operator had told the pilot that they were on the same course as the bomber, the pilot could sort out where this light section was and tell his operator where he wanted to be for the closing stages of the interception.

Of course there were nights when visibility was exceptionally good and one might obtain a visual at 3,000 or 4,000 feet. This was usually in conditions of bright moonlight, and the Hun usually avoided raiding on such occasions.

What it boiled down to was that the operator had to pick up a contact on his A.I. tubes, interpret what it was doing, give the pilot instructions which would enable him to intercept the target, and at the same time give him the fullest possible indication of where he should look for the target.

The pilot, for his part, had to fly the aircraft extremely accurately on instruments in the dark and then, when he was actually trying to see the target, he must fly completely by instinct. When it is remembered that an enemy bomber would probably not fly straight and level and that there were all sorts of little things that could go wrong with various bits of equipment, it will be realised that a tremendous amount of practice was essential before a crew could work together efficiently as a team.

The flight starting a two-day tour of duty would assemble in the morning at dispersal for training, either in the form of lectures and discussions or flying practice. In the afternoon all aircraft that were to fly that night would be thoroughly tested in the air. They would take off in twos, the pilots checking their engines on the ground and during the climb; the R/T would be tested on all channels, the intercom between pilot and operator checked, oxygen switched on to see that the supply was working, and finally the two aircraft would manoeuvre in order to carry out some practice interceptions which would also check the A.I.

These daylight interceptions during a night-flying test run were usually carried out at a height of about 14,000 feet. It has already been seen that the range of A.I. Mark 4 was limited by the height above ground. The maximum range attainable, regardless of what height the aircraft flew, was about 14,000 feet, so that by carrying out N.F.T.s at that height the A.I. could be checked for maximum range. During daylight interceptions it was essential for the pilot to resist the temptation to cheat, even if his operator managed to get himself in the most awful tangle. When the attempted interception was finished, he could tell his operator where he had gone wrong, but if he corrected the operator's errors, either instinctively or knowingly, the crew missed the opportunity of learning from these mistakes.

When the crew was considered far enough advanced to attempt interceptions at night, there was no chance of cheating, but it was amazing how long it took some pilots to realise the importance of carrying out the daylight exercises conscientiously.

Once the N.F.T. had been completed, crews would go off to their respective messes for a meal and then report back to dispersal half an hour before official black-out time. A night state would have been prepared by the Flight Commander which would show the names of the crews on readiness, in the order in which they would be called on to take off if required. They would, of course, fly the same aircraft they had tested in the afternoon.

Any pilots still lacking Beau flying hours would be sent off for dusk circuits and bumps. If the weather was good, and if Sector approved, two Beaus would go off for practice. The remaining crews would sit around listening to the more experienced chaps nattering about this and that. The cards would appear for bridge or poker. Books were read, letters written and a pleasant time would be had by all. I found it most interesting to listen to what the old hands had to say. I certainly picked up many useful tips.

During August I flew as often in Defiants as in Beaus, but by the end of the month all the Defiants had gone. My log book shows that I had seventeen flights that month and flew with ten different pilots. After that, however, the crewing problems were sorted out and crews flew together whenever possible. It had been realised how important team work would be, and it became Fighter Command policy to try to keep a crew together for their entire operational career.

I had been on probation for a month and at the beginning of September I became a sergeant. I was presented with my flying brevet by the Flight Commander, and it was a very proud moment for me when I stitched the single wing brevet on my tunic. This brevet bore the letters 'RO', short for Radio Observer, but at a later stage it was decided to do away with the 'RO' and the old 'O' or Observer brevet and to replace them with 'N' for Navigator, though on night fighters we were always referred to as Navigators Radio or N/Rs. In order to avoid confusion, I will refer to myself and my fellow knob twiddlers as Navigators.

Lofty Hamer did not yet have enough flying hours on Beaus to take one up at night so that most of our September flying was carried out in daylight. We did many homings and worked our way through the set exercises that had been evolved for A.I. training. I found Lofty to be extremely painstaking in carrying out these exercises and very patient indeed with me. Towards the end of the month he had sufficient Beau flying time to be set off on dusk landings, and when he had made a couple of successful solo landings I was allowed to join him for our first night trip together. By the end of September I had forty-two hours of day-flying and two hours of night in my log book.

On the morning of October 3rd I flew with Flight Lieutenant Waddingham, the Deputy Flight Commander. He flew with each of the navigators of the flight to see how they were getting on with A.I. and to sort out the geese from the swans. We took off with another Beau as 'playmate', to operate under G.C.I. control.

The aircraft plot displayed on the operations table at Sector Headquarters was made up from information received from the long-range warning radar, supplemented by Observer Corps reports and plots from new ground radar stations called Ground Control Interception Stations, or G.C.I.s for short. They were mainly concerned with the affairs of their own Group. These G.C.I. stations were the answer to the last of the problems that had beset the early night fighters. The best that the Sector controller had been able to do was to bring a fighter to within five or six miles of a bomber. This was not enough even for the A.I.-equipped fighters. The Mark 4 A.I. sets had a maximum range of only three or four miles. A G.C.I. Controller, with his new ground radar equipment, could now bring the fighter much closer to its quarry, certainly to within one or two miles, depending on the proficiency of the G.C.I. Controller and how well his apparatus was working.

Just as the Beau crews needed intensive practice with A.I., so did the G.C.I. Controllers with their equipment; collaboration became the keynote of an association that was to be most profitable for all concerned. When they were first introduced, G.C.I. stations were capable of controlling only one fighter at a time, but it was not long before multiple control positions were made possible.

The trip with Flight Lieutenant Waddingham went off very well on the whole. Once the G.C.I. Controller took us over he gave us a vector; that is to say, a course on which to fly. At the same time he gave us as much information as he could about the aircraft we were chasing, its height, range and the course it was steering relative to us.

As the range closed to four miles, I knew that I should soon see the target on my A.I., but, search as I might, I could see nothing even faintly resembling an aircraft blip.

'He's only two miles from you now. Crossing starboard to port about the same level. Any joy?' asked the Controller anxiously.

'I can't see a thing on the set,' I told my pilot, hoping desperately that it was not my mishandling of the A.I. that was the reason for the target's blip not appearing.

Much to my relief he replied: 'My ruddy eyeballs are just about popping out looking for the darned thing and I can't see it. Hullo! Just a moment, there's a Beau way above us, going away to port. I expect that's him. He's about a mile behind us and at least four thousand feet above. They'll have to do a darned sight better than that.'

We had gone on to intercom, so my pilot switched back to R/T and told the Controller what had happened. He expressed his apologies and sent both Beaus off for another attempt. This was just as unsuccessful as the first try, but at the third attempt everything worked perfectly. The contact appeared on my A.I. just as the Controller's instructions and information indicated that it should. For my part, I managed to complete the interception without too many boobs.

The other Beau was then given a couple of runs which I watched, looking through my Perspex dome as it manoeuvred into position behind us. It was lovely and sunny up at 15,000 feet and I could see the other Beau, a tiny black dot against a few scattered white clouds, below us and about six or seven miles out to starboard.

Sometimes the cloud formations were breathtakingly beautiful. Although I became a bit blasé about flying after a while, I always found night flying thrilling, while during the day the excitements were mostly confined to low flying or buzzing through the tops of clouds which formed a strange world of uncanny beauty.

We had a lot to discuss when we landed. It was obvious that the combination of G.C.I. and A.I. could work but a great deal of co-operation and practice would be necessary. We had found that the main weakness of G.C.I. was the question of sorting out the height of the target aircraft. The reason for this was that the early G.C.I. equipment did not have its own height-finder and had to rely on the rather inaccurate heights passed through normal control. It was not long before this weakness was corrected.

I was most surprised to find that we had been airborne over two and a half hours. The time had simply flown. This was something I always found when operating A.I.; it was so interesting to use and the challenge it offered was so intriguing that I never became bored with it. It seemed to defy mastery — as if it were a crossword puzzle with the ability to change all its clues just as the last two or three words were being filled in.

Early in October 1941 I found myself one of four navigators who were asked if we would like to be put up for commissions. All four of us gladly accepted the offer and we were told that it was most unlikely that the recommendations would be refused by the Air Ministry. It was expected that the commissions would take about three months to come through.

One unforeseen development from this was that I learned that I would be recrewed with one of the officers in 'B' Flight who was crewed with an N.C.O. not up for a commission. I had been getting on very well with Lofty Hamer, both on the ground and in the air. Although I felt that I would miss his quiet, matter-of-fact ways, I realised that team work was going

38

to be so important on this night-fighter business that it was obviously right that a crew should share the same mess.

I found that Lofty agreed with this. He had twice been offered a commission but had turned the offer down. He had been a senior N.C.O. for some time and preferred life in the sergeants' mess. Many N.C.O.s felt the same way as he did and it was nothing to hold against him.

Chapter III

NEW PARTNERSHIP

MY new pilot was Flying Officer James Ghilles Benson, an experienced flyer who had one victory to his credit already. Of the considerable amount of good luck that came my way during the war, perhaps my crewing with Ben was the luckiest thing of all. With the exception of five months in 1943, we were to remain as a crew until we came off operations in 1945. In all the three and a half years that we flew together we did not have a single row or argument in spite of frustrations, near disasters, postings, blunders and the hundred and one little incidents bound to occur during hours of operational flying.

The outstanding things about Ben were his personality, his power of leadership, his ability to get on with the job in hand whatever it might be, and his sense of humour. He had a deep sense of responsibility; so far as I could see, he was quite fearless, as keen as mustard and quite unflappable. Whilst I was learning my job he was patience itself, particularly in the early stages when neither of us could be sure if our failures were due to me or to the equipment. We both made mistakes, but learned never to make the same mistake twice. He was an excellent and painstaking pilot, and from our first flight together I had complete confidence in him. I knew that he would give me every bit of help possible to prove my capabilities, and, once I had done so, he reciprocated my confidence in him without either of us having to put anything into words.

When I came to write this part of the book I realised that,

although I had known that Ben had considerable flying experience before I crewed up with him, I had only a vague idea of what that experience amounted to. I knew he had been on 141 Squadron for some time and that he already had one victory to his credit, but that was about all I did know.

He is now an executive with one of the big petrol concerns. I wrote to him, explaining the position and asking him to fill in the details of his earlier R.A.F. career. He was kind enough to oblige. I found that his story brings out the frustrations, trials and tribulations of those early days of night fighting so well that I have left it as he told it.

*   *   *   *

I left the Flying Training School at Montrose in July 1940. Looking back on it, I see that I was assessed as an above-average pilot. This may have been a disadvantage as it turned out later, for it was probably thought that pilots with this classification should be given the more complicated role of night fighting rather than day fighting, which was a bit of a hit-and-miss affair.

From there I went to Aston Down, which was a Fighter Training School. The main attraction there was that it was manned by the entire remnants of Number 1 Squadron, which had just returned from France. The outstanding feature at Aston Down, apart from the regular crashes that occurred because of its smallness, was the remarkable aerobatics of Number 1 Squadron whenever there was a serviceable aircraft to fly. They included two well-known aerobatics demonstrators among their members, one of whom showed his ability by shooting down an enemy aircraft over the airfield one day with a Spitfire out of the training wing. This was regarded as a pretty good feat at the time.

I left there on July 25th and reported to 141 Squadron, where I was told that I was a replacement for one of the eleven pilots who had been shot down the previous week. The squadron had left West Malling to patrol a convoy in mid-Channel when some Messerschmitt 110s had attacked them from up sun. Only one pilot had got back to West Malling. Because the squadron had few aircraft and fewer pilots, it was retired to Grangemouth to re-equip.

The aircraft we were flying were Defiants, and in August we were put on day-fighter duties, with detachments at Grangemouth, Dyce and Turnhouse, on the east coast of Scotland. Although we did quite a lot of flying, we never saw an enemy aircraft, and the nearest we got to an attack was when we tried to shoot down a Lockheed Hudson which had become mixed up with an enemy raid. Fortunately this did not come off!

As it had been decided that the squadron would probably go on to night fighting, we moved to the Edinburgh area to do some night-flying training, which was sadly lacking at that time. When I look back now at the meagre facilities available for night flying at that time, it seems strange to realise the fantastic difficulties put in the path of anybody trying to operate in an aircraft at night.

We were flying from grass airfields with no runways. The maximum number of lights allowed at first was six 'glim' lamps which certainly showed only a glimmer of light. These were the only lights available for both take-off and landing. There was little or no help to be had from Flying Control, and this, coupled with the fact that at that time we had very poor radios which were all too liable to pack up, made life and training in general fairly exciting.

In October 1940 I was with a detachment moved to Gatwick. Two of the pilots had some success, although the problems of flying at night in the ack-ack zone were considerable. We were still in Defiants and my gunner was a chap by the name of Blane. During October we were sent to Biggin Hill to cover night-flying operations.

The difficulties were enormous. I will always remember my first night patrol from Biggin Hill. I took off with the aid of the six glim-lamps, which were immediately extinguished as I went into the air. The airfield was being bombed at the time. I was shot at by the airfield defences as I took off, coned by searchlights soon after and then got lost in cloud, only to find that

42

my radio had packed up!

I had been told that if I was lost I should look for a blue searchlight. Never having seen a searchlight from the air before, I found that they all looked blue as I approached them. To my horror, however, each time I tried to get a homing from one of them, I was coned or followed around.

I decided that it would be safer in cloud, despite the fact that I was completely lost. On this particular evening we had the distinguished experience of flying right through the London balloon barrage, which we fortunately did not see. Then we sighted an enemy aircraft, which we chased but lost in cloud. We were only rescued from the necessity of having to bale out by the action of a brave man at Gatwick Airport. He turned on the flashing beacon in the middle of an air raid, thereby enabling us to do a rather dicey landing there.

This sort of thing happened pretty frequently, so the squadron worked out a homing system. Immediately you found you were lost, you flew twenty minutes due south until you calculated you were over the Channel. You then went down gently until you were below cloud, flew up and down until you found the two piers at Brighton and if you headed north from half-way between the piers you would see the signal lights on a railway. You had to remember that it went down through a tunnel or a deep cutting through the South Downs, but you could follow it to Gatwick. If you could not get in there, you followed the railway line to Croydon airfield. That was closed at night, but if you turned hard left and took the Purley line, you would probably see Kenley, where they might be kind enough to let you land.

One of our sergeant pilots did this one night in thick fog. He was unable to see anything at Gatwick. He carried on to Croydon, hugging the railway, then turned hard left, keeping at nought feet in order not to loose sight of it. When he thought he had just about reached Kenley, he called them up and asked them to put on their flashing beacon. It came on at once. What worried him was that it was actually flashing above him!

We had some desperate nights in December of that year,

43

patrolling over the centre of London during the Blitz, trying to pick out German bombers against the glow of the fires. On these occasions we had to fly with the cockpit hood open without any indication as to the height of the raiders. The nearest we got to one was when we nearly had a head-on collision with a Heinkel going in the opposite direction. Unfortunately, the closing speed was so fast we could not get in a shot. We did, in fact, see a tremendous amount of London burning during the 8th and 10th of December, but there was nothing very constructive we could do about it.

It is interesting to note that on December 11th we were sent on what must have been one of the very first Intruder patrols over France. We went the whole way to Abbeville, searching around at various altitudes for returning German bombers. We did not see any but had the satisfaction of shooting at some glasshouses that were reflecting the moonlight. This was quite an adventurous trip really for a single-engined Defiant, especially as we had no navigational aids and very indifferent radio at that time.

On December 22nd we managed to get off on a reasonably early patrol. We sighted a Heinkel high above us, crossing over the Sussex coast, and eventually shot it down.

About a week later we were returning to Gravesend after a long patrol, and as we made our approach to land we were mistaken for a German bomber. To our horror the glim-lamps were extinguished just as we were coming in and we suddenly found ourselves in fog at nought feet. We hit a dispersal bay and crashed where the runway would have been – if there had been such things in those days. We were very lucky to survive really, as our wheels were taken right off by the dispersal bay. Although Blane, who was flying with me, suffered a broken nose and I had concussion and lacerations to my head, we were both keen enough to be able to be operational within three weeks. Really, I suppose, we should have been satisfactorily dead!

Be that as it may, it set us back for the rest of the month, but we returned to operational flying in February 1941, and continued through the heavy Blitzes of March, when we saw a great deal of the City burning. We were patrolling over London during one of the worst raids at the end of March and I remember seeing almost the whole of Thameshaven on fire. Our luck was out though; it was almost impossible to see a Hun by just looking out of an aircraft unless you knew where to look.

We operated from Manston on the odd occasion and that was a very exciting place to be. It was right in the thick of it all. Without A.I. or reasonable radio sets, success was very hard to come by for the squadron. We did see another Heinkel over London on April 17th, but we were unable to get a shot at it. At the end of that month we went north to Ayr for re-equipping, feeling that although we had had some excitement, we really had not earned our keep.

When I look back on those months in the south it really is very hard to realise just how difficult it was to try to operate aircraft at night during that period. At that stage of the war the chief task confronting anybody who took off at night was to try and get himself and his aircraft back safely on the ground. The accident rate was extremely high. Many people got lost and had to spend most of their time in the air trying to find out where they were.

The accent at this time was, not unnaturally, on day-fighter activities. The airfields were frequently being bombed and were resolutely averse to showing any illumination at night whatsoever. If you had to take off from a day-fighter base for a night patrol they were very pleased to see you go and did not want to see you landing back there again.

There were no means for recognition of our night fighters by searchlights and ack-ack. There seemed to be no planned patrols, and wherever you went you were fired at, illuminated and coned as if you were an enemy aircraft. It was all very exciting, but it did not help you to attack enemy bombers. Nobody at this time had any night-fighting experience and very few people had much experience in flying at night in adverse weather conditions.

On the Newcastle coast, where we next appeared, there were

45

a few targets to be chased up. In May we experienced the ignominy of being fired at by an enemy aircraft whose presence we had not even suspected. Unfortunately it disappeared and we did not have a chance of getting our own back. There was another piece of excitement that month when we had an engine failure while we were up in a Defiant. When that happens in a single-engined aircraft you just have to land without one. We did this, landing at Acklington and damaging the aircraft severely.

The squadron had a certain amount of success at this time, catching several German bombers in raids on Newcastle. I did not have the good fortune to find anything, however. We continued with the good work until July and August 1941, when we started converting to Blenheims and subsequently to Beaufighters, when no doubt, your story begins.

*   *   *   *

The only comment I will make on Ben's story is that it underlines the point I have already made of my amazing good luck in getting on to night fighting just at the psychological time when nearly every one of the difficulties connected with flying at night had been overcome.

So far as Ben was concerned, he had a fine twin-engined Beau to fly. It was fitted with Very High Frequency R/T, which worked supremely well. Airfields used for night fighting now had good lighting and runways with an efficient Flying Control. Patrols were properly planned and there was an excellent liaison between searchlights, guns and aircraft.

The only new equipment whose usefulness and reliability still had to be tested and proved was A.I. It was my job to make this work, and I found that Ben was at all times patient, helpful and co-operative.

The first three months Ben and I were together were spent in practice, practice and more practice. We sorted out what seemed to us the best mixture of directions and information for me to pass on to Ben, so that I would have control of the interception whilst giving him as clear a picture as possible of what

46

was taking place. Some pilots insisted that the navigator should just give a running commentary of what the target aircraft was doing and leave the pilot to carry out the interception. It was obvious to us both that this method did not get the fullest benefit from A.I., so we stuck to our own ideas.

We found out what a pernickety, temperamental piece of equipment A.I. could be. After all, it was fairly fragile stuff to be installed in an aircraft and flown around the sky. The vibration of the engines, the inevitable bounces, great or small according to the pilot's skill in landing, the surges in power from the engines, all these could cause faults. Then we found that A.I. could squint. If one aerial was not as efficient as its opposite number, a false picture would be presented on the cathode ray tubes. We learned to watch for this on the night-flying tests, which were always carried out in daylight. I would bring Ben in behind our target so that it appeared dead ahead and level at a range of about a thousand feet and he would tell me exactly where the other aircraft was. It did not always squint, of course, but if it did we could allow for that at night. The really difficult time could arise, however, when a fault occurred in an aerial after the night-flying test had been carried out. As the aerials were rather allergic to damp, these faults were not infrequent.

Number 141 Squadron had been detailed to keep three Beaus at Drem, near Edinburgh, and crews took it in turns to spend three nights there. Ben and I went there in October and again in December, and each time we were ordered off for an operational patrol. Both times there were some Huns about but much too far south, though the time was not wasted as we practised with the local G.C.I.

Early in January 1942 Ben and I were sent on attachment to 29 Squadron at West Malling Kent. They had quite a bit of operational experience and we were to pick up any hints and advice that we could. At the same time Flight Lieutenant Braham and his navigator, 29 Squadron's most successful crew, had a similar attachment to our squadron to natter to our crews and answer questions. Interchange of information of this sort was extremely useful, and Fighter Command were to be congratulated on remembering its importance right through the war.

Unfortunately for us, the weather was so bad for the few days that we were at West Malling that no night flying was carried out at all. We would dearly have loved a crack at the Hun, but we had to contain our impatience. For me, at any rate, there was some compensation in the kick I received every time I flew at night. Even when we were off on practice interceptions there was something about clambering into the Beau in the dark that made me tingle with excitement.

In the Beau, feeling bulky with flying kit, I would strap myself in the seat under the Perspex dome and swivel myself round so as to face the front to watch the take-off. First one powerful Hercules engine, then the other, would roar into life as the ground crew plugged the starter battery in. Ben would rev up the engines and the aircraft would surge forward against the chocks. A signal from Ben and the chocks were hauled away. We would taxi around the perimeter track to the end of the runway in use – landing and take-off were always made into the wind – then a final run-up of the engines against the brakes for Ben to check oil and air pressures on both engines. A final 'Okay' from Air Traffic Control and, with a roar of engines, we would gather speed as we moved along the runway with a second or two of tension as the Beau lurched off into the air. Then Ben would snatch at the lever that retracted the undercarriage and we were airborne. A wide sweep around the airfield, then we would leave its few, friendly lights as we climbed up to our operational height.

Once I became moderately competent with A.I. there was the thrill of the chase, even if it was only another Beau that we were after: to use the wonderful apparatus we had been given and, when everything had worked well, to hear Ben say:

'Okay. There she is now. Turn round and have a look.'

It was always exciting to see the shadowy silhouette of a Beau just in front of us and to know that if it had been a Hun we had the power to blow it out of the sky. And almost every flight gave me that thrill not just once but several times.

Most crews were beginning to think that it was about time that we began to put all this practice and theory into real operational use, and we found to our joy that 141 Squadron was to move to Acklington on January 28th. Admittedly, most of the action was to be found in south-eastern England, but Acklington was a front-line station and we might expect some action there. It was an added kick for me to return to the station where a few short months ago I had been a lowly erk.

With 141 Squadron at Acklington there was a day-fighter squadron and a Turbinlite flight; we did not see much of the day squadron as we were off duty when they were on and *vice versa*. We did see quite a bit of the Turbinlites, though – almost too much.

In the desperate days when every plausible idea was seized upon to combat the night bomber someone had suggested an airborne searchlight. The Douglas Havoc had been selected as the aircraft in which to mount a searchlight, complete with batteries to operate it. When all the necessary equipment was fitted into the Havoc, it was found that there was no room for guns, so out they came. Obviously a searchlight up in the sky was of no use unless guns could operate with it, so it was decided that one or two Hurricanes should take off with the Turbinlite Havoc and formate on it with the assistance of lights in the trailing edge of the Havoc's wing. It had also been found that Mark 4 A.I. would fit into the Havoc, so in it went.

The idea was that the Turbinlite would intercept a bomber, illuminate it with his searchlight and the Hurricanes would dive in to shoot down the blinded bomber. Unfortunately the whole operation was much too unwieldy to operate successfully. On the few occasions when an enemy bomber was illuminated, it escaped from the searchlight beam before the fighter could get close enough to fire, and once the bomber was out of the beam the fighter could do nothing. No enemy bombers were shot down by the Turbinlite fighters, and there was a rumour that a Halifax had been attacked by them on a dark night.

Once the A.I. equipped Beaufighter appeared on the scene it could do all that the cumbersome Turbinlite set-up could without forfeiting the element of surprise that was the night fighter's main asset. Several flights of Turbinlites had been formed and many useful trained night-fighter crews were tied up in this operation for over a year. The powers-that-be certainly persisted far too long with Turbinlites.

Ben and I were rather fed up to hear that 141 Squadron still had to maintain the detachment at Drem and we were sent there with two other crews for a week from January 30th. We gnashed our teeth at the thought that no sooner had we been moved to an operational station, than we were promptly whisked off it. We dreaded to hear of all the excitement we were missing, and the weather was so bad at Drem that we only got one night trip in the whole week. When we returned, however, we found that the weather had been even worse at Acklington and there had been no excitement apart from frantic snow clearing on the runways and wondering if Acklington was going to be isolated by the heavy snowfall.

Ben was due for ten days' leave and departed southwards as soon as we returned to Acklington. The weather remained pretty foul but I managed to do a night-flying test run one afternoon, followed with a two-hour G.C.I. exercise that night, both trips with Lofty Hamer as pilot. Four days later I had two similar flights with one of Ben's particular friends, Flight Lieutenant Ivor Cosby. All these flights were without any special incident, though we were all getting very keyed up.

Ben and 'Koz' had been together on the squadron for some time, and when the two of them got together in the mess things began to happen. Koz had a sense of humour much like Ben's, so they made a good pair. I am afraid that nicknames on the squadron were rather lacking in imagination, usually being just an abbreviation of the first syllable of the surname. Thus I became 'Brandy', for the rest of my Service career.

By the time Ben returned from leave there had been one spot of excitement when two aircraft of 'A' Flight had been scrambled one night to meet a threatened raid that did not materialise. Our Flight was starting a two-day spell on duty, so that afternoon we went off for our N.F.T. in Beaufighter

Number 7577, which had been allocated to us to fly whenever it was available. It was as well if a crew could stick to the same aircraft as much as possible and get to know its idiosyncrasies.

We had been told that the latest practice of the Hun, especially when raiding coastal targets, was to drop his bombs from anything up to twenty thousand feet and then stick his nose down in as fast a dive for home as possible. On this particular N.F.T. we arranged for the target to carry out these tactics, while I tried to follow him on A.I. It was difficult, but it could be done; correct speed control was the main worry.

Chapter IV

FIRST BLOOD

ON the night of February 15th we arrived at dispersal to find that we were fifth crew due to fly on the Night State list. It was a fine evening and two aircraft were sent off on a dusk patrol which would consist of G.C.I. controlled practice interceptions a little way off the East Coast, where they would be in a good position if anything did come in from the Fatherland.

During the war the Services worked on a twenty-four hour clock time. That is to say, there was no a.m. and p.m.; one p.m. became thirteen hundred hours, or '13.00', and so on.

At about 18.45 hours the Flight Commander spoke to the Sector Controller on the ops telephone and suggested relieving the pair of Beaus then airborne with a fresh pair, as they had been up almost two hours. As he put the telephone down, all eyes were on him, as if we sensed that there was something doing.

'They are keeping 27 and 32 up for a while and they want two more off. There may be something doing.'

The two crews next off on the Night State were out of the door almost before he had finished speaking. Ben and I, who would be next off after them were really straining at the leash. For ten minutes we were kept in suspense, then the ops telephone rang.

'Off you go. Two more. You are to go straight over to Sector Control as soon as you have made enough height to get them on R/T.'

The Flight Commander was last off on the Night State. I could imagine how he was cursing his luck at being on the ground while there was something happening. I hoped we would not be too late for some action.

Meanwhile, we had grabbed our bits and pieces and were well on the way to our Beau. We clambered in and went through the usual procedure. This time it was the real thing. Soon we were taxying round the perimeter track. I had checked the cannons, then strapped myself in my seat and plugged in the lead from my helmet for the R/T and intercom. Oxygen was switched on; we used oxygen from take-off at night.

By this time we were at the end of the runway, with the other Beau just discernible behind us.

'All set?' asked Ben. 'Right then. Away we go.'

Away he went, down the runway, then climbing as fast as the Beau could reasonably go. Ben had an eight-channel R/T set with push-button control. As soon as we had climbed enough, he pressed the appropriate button for Sector Control.

'Hello, Homestead. Hello, Homestead. Rounder three-six. What instructions, please?'

'Hello, Rounder three-six. Vector zero four five. What are your angels?'

This means: 'Steer a course of 045 degrees. What height are you?'

'Hello, Homestead. Three-six steering zero four five, angels seven still climbing.'

'Hello, three-six. Continue climbing to angels fourteen on present course.'

It was a dark night, with a fair amount of low cloud, the tops of which were about one thousand five hundred feet. Up where we were, however, it was clear. We passed over the coast and saw that we were about eight miles north of Blyth. A few minutes later we were given a southerly course to steer and were told to go over to the G.C.I. control.

Ben pressed another button and gave our call sign to the Controller. We knew that at that time the G.C.I. Controller could handle only one interception at a time. He already had a

Beau under control on another channel and we were being kept handy until the other interception was completed.

We could see the bursting anti-aircraft shells high over Sunderland – so that was where the trouble was.

'Hello, Rounder three-six. This is Blackbird. Continue on present course, we may have something for you. What are your angels?'

'Good show! Angels one-four. Listening out.'

Apart from a few hurried peeps through my Perspex dome when Ben pointed something out to me, my eyes had been glued to the rubber visor through which I was peering hopefully at the cathode ray tubes of the A.I. Suddenly I noticed a tenuous blip which just crept out of the ground returns at maximum range and then lost itself again in the grounds as the aircraft which had caused it went out of range again.

'Contact!' I yelled to Ben through the intercom. 'It's gone now. I only had it for a second but I'm sure it was an aircraft.'

'Which way did it go?' asked Ben plaintively.

'Didn't have time to see,' I replied. 'Still, I'm sure it was an aircraft.'

'I'll get on to the Controller,' said Ben.

'Hello, Blackbird. This is Rounder three-six. Is there anyone near me?'

'Rounder three-six. Blackbird here. Hard port on to zero eight zero. It looks like a Bandit going home. It's well below you.'

Ben swung the heavy nose round and put her nose down. As he did so, he opened the throttles and she fairly hurled herself after the Bandit. The Beau was capable of about three hundred miles an hour and probably thirty more in a dive. We were doing all of three hundred and thirty miles an hour as we screamed down.

'Any joy yet?' Ben was asking.

But for two or three minutes there was nothing to see, though my eyes were straining to the utmost. Then, coming very slowly out of the ground returns, a blip emerged.

'Contact! Gently starboard. Keep going down.'

'Ah-h-h!' breathed Ben as the aircraft responded immediately to my instructions. 'Keep hold of the blighter.'

'Steady now. It's dead ahead about three miles. What height are we and can you go any faster?'

'Height is nine thousand five hundred and we're going balls out already. Are we catching him?'

But the sad fact was that we were not gaining on him at all.

It was only the extra speed we had gathered in the dive that had brought us closer to him. As soon as our height coincided with his and I had told Ben to level out, I had the mortification of seeing the blip slowly slide up the time base and out of range.

Ben called Blackbird Control to tell him that we had lost contact and we were informed that our target was drawing right away from us. It must have been going like a bat out of hell.

To say we were disappointed was an understatement. If only the wretched Controller had been able to tackle more than one interception at a time we might have had some joy.

The Controller brought us back almost over Acklington, then the excitement started all over again.

'Hello, Rounder three-six. Blackbird Control. We have a Bogey for you to investigate. Turn port on to zero one zero. Range five miles.'

The term Bogey meant we had to identify with extra care as it might be a friendly aircraft. Bandit meant that it was almost certainly an enemy. In either case positive identification was essential.

'Hello, three-six. Range now four miles, crossing you port to starboard. Any joy yet?'

'No, nothing yet,' I informed Ben.

A second or two later it was a different story. A quite firm blip showed on both tubes, over to port and slightly below.

'Contact!' I called over the intercom. 'Gently port and go down. Range three and a half miles.'

As Ben responded at once to my instructions he informed the Controller that we had contact.

'Do you require any further help?' asked the Controller.

'Ease the turn now. Range three miles. No, I don't need any more help,' I told Ben.

He passed that information to the Controller and we went on to intercom. I could see that the aircraft we were chasing was still slightly over to port but the blip was slowly moving across the time base to starboard. We were flying straight now, so he was crossing us from port to starboard as the Controller had said. I could anticipate this and cut him off by turning now.

'Gently starboard. Range two and a half miles,' I told Ben.

'Gently starboard. I'm still going down.'

'Level out now. . . . Keep going starboard.'

Thank the Lord he had reminded me of the height; I had been watching the azimuth tube too closely and had forgotten to watch the elevation tube.

As we levelled out, Ben automatically opened the throttles slightly to keep our speed constant. We were closing in perfectly. The blip showed almost dead ahead now.

'Steady now. . . . Range one and a half. . . . We're coming in nicely. Where do you want him?'

'Steady. Put him starboard and above. About ten degrees starboard. What range now?'

'Just under a mile. Throttle back slightly. Can you see anything yet?'

'No, not yet. Keep giving me the range.'

'About two thousand feet. Gently port now.'

A moment's pause, then explosively: 'Christ! There it is. It's a bloody great Dornier. Here, have a look. I can hold it now.'

I needed no urging but swivelled my seat around and peered into the blackness. My eyes took a moment to become accustomed to the dark, then I saw, just above and to starboard of us, the vague silhouette of an aircraft with pinpoints of reddish lights showing from the exhausts. I could see the pencil-slim fuselage and the twin fins. It was a Dornier 217, all right. Ben, who by this time was formating immediately beneath the Dornier and was only two or three hundred feet below, decided that time for action had arrived.

The Dornier was weaving gently from side to side as it flew

along. Ben throttled back very slightly and lifted the nose of the Beau. It was a little over to port now. It seemed strange that it should be completely indifferent to the presence of a Beaufighter so close. As it drifted across in front of us, my heart was thumping so loudly it seemed impossible for the Huns not to hear it. As it passed through his gunsight, Ben turned the Beau almost imperceptibly to follow the Dornier. All hell broke loose as he pressed the gun button and four cannons and six machineguns banged and chattered away. The Beau filled with the acrid smoke and smell of cordite.

Ben had given it a two-second burst of gunfire; but although the Dornier began to loose height, we had seen no strikes. We did not use tracer bullets at night in order to retain the element of surprise. We were now following it down in a very sharp dive and Ben gave it two more short bursts from about three hundred feet range. This time we saw strikes all along the fuselage and tail unit, from which there was a great red flash which illumined the whole aircraft.

Ben was having a devil of a job to keep behind it now. We kept getting into the slipstream which threw us about violently. Before Ben could get another burst in, the Dornier had entered the clouds, diving into them at a very steep angle. We were about a thousand feet behind it by then and at a height of only two thousand feet Ben pulled out of the dive. We circled the spot where we had last seen the Dornier, hoping that we might see an explosion as it hit the deck. No such luck.

We called Control to report and to ask if there was anything else for us. All was quiet now, though, and we were given a vector for Acklington. As I guided Ben home, we discussed the night's events.

'I wonder if the other chaps had any luck,' I mused.

'Oh, I should think so,' replied Ben. There must have been quite a few Huns around. What bloody bad luck though. I'm sure our Dornier must have gone in, but the best we will be given is a Probable, more likely we'll only get a Damaged. I should have got the damned thing with that first burst. Ah well!'

We were soon back at base, and when we taxied into our dispersal bay our jubilant ground crew were waiting to welcome us. The Flight Commander and the intelligence Officer were also awaiting us. Although there had been several chases, we were told, ours had been the only combat.

In the crew-room we were just taking off our flying clothing when the ops telephone rang. It was the Sector Controller to congratulate us and to tell us the glad news that the Royal Observer Corps and Saint Mary's Lighthouse had independently reported a plane crashing into the sea four miles east of Blyth.

There had been no other combats; the guns were not claiming anything and the time and place coincided with our combat. We were told, therefore, that we could claim the Dornier as destroyed.

Soon after we had landed, the weather deteriorated. Sector decided that it was most unlikely that there would be any further activity that night, and so we were stood down except for two crews. The rest of us made our way to our respective messes and indulged in a beer or two.

Next morning I was sitting down to my bacon and egg in the sergeants' mess, feeling very bucked with the thought that we had opened the Squadron's A.I. score on our first really operational sortie. The radio was switched on for the news and I had the great satisfaction of hearing:

'A small force of enemy bombers attacked towns in the north of England last night. A Dornier 217 was shot down by one of our night fighters.'

The bad weather remained with us for the next few days so that we managed to do only one night flight. There was no enemy activity but we carried out some useful G.C.I. runs. Ben also had some air-firing practice, shooting at a drogue towed by another aircraft. Again we smelt that gunsmoke.

On February 21st my commission came through and I was sent off on a week's leave to London to fix myself up with an officer's uniform and kit. Luckily, I had been recommended to a first-class tailor in Sackville Street. Not only did he complete the whole business, including fittings, in five days but he did it all for the rather meagre sum allowed by Air Ministry. It all fitted perfectly and I still have the greatcoat he made for me. I had fourteen years' wear from it in the R.A.F. and it is in very good shape even now.

Greatcoat, raincoat, best blues, two shirts, four collars, three pairs of socks, a pair of shoes and a tie had cost somewhere in the region of twenty-four pounds – and all the kit was absolutely first class.

I returned to Acklington on the last day of February. One of the first persons I saw was the Flight Sergeant in charge of the guard-room, where, less than a year before, I had been one of his policemen. As he whipped me up a smart salute I could hardly restrain a delighted grin; we had all moved in fear and trembling of this particular chappie.

Acklington was miles from anywhere, and probably for that reason there was always a very pleasant atmosphere in the officers' mess. We had to make our own entertainment, but we made life very enjoyable there, largely with the air of a radio-gram and some of the latest records. There was a comfortable little bar, and a civilian mess secretary saw to it that the mess was well run and the food appetising. The squadron officers were a grand bunch and the station officers helpful and friendly. In spite of its geographical position Acklington was a pretty good station to be on.

There had been a bitterly cold spell of weather at the end of February which lasted well into March. There were fairly heavy falls of snow and I well remember cycling round the perimeter track of the airfield on my way to dispersal and being very nearly blown off my bicycle by a howling gale. It was freezing cold and snowing hard. Being almost on the East Coast, it was very exposed to the east wind. As I neared dispersal I noticed airmen working on several Beaus parked in the open. It is difficult to imagine a worse job than working under these conditions on metal aircraft. Usually the engine fitters had to work with bare hands; at best they could wear mittens. In spite of all this they were always cheerful and terrifically keen.

It was easy enough for the aircrews to keep up a good squadron spirit; but in my experience, on all the squadrons with which I served the spirit of the ground crews and their willingness to work at all hours and under the most disheartening conditions really had to be seen to be believed. I do not believe that sufficient praise can ever be given to the ground crews in the R.A.F., particularly to those on night-fighter squadrons, for the truly magnificent job they did.

As far as possible the ground crews were assigned to their own particular aircraft – and what a pride they would take in it. Our Beau had hardly landed after our combat before the ground crew had a swastika painted on. Later, when Ben and I were on 157 Squadron, we arrived at dispersal one morning to find our Mosquito had been christened Queen of the Skies by our ground crew. They always made sure, to the best of their ability, that she lived up to her name.

It was during this extremely cold spell that I received a letter from one of the chaps who had been with me at Scarborough. He had not fancied trying for night fighters because he had always been interested in pure navigation. He had been sent to the United States for his training and had actually been on the first navigators' course to be held there. As I shivered at Acklington, I read the address on the top right-hand side of his letter:

Coral Gables, Palm Springs, Miami, Florida.

The March weather remained bad and it was not until near the end of the month that the snow began to clear. After our experience with G.C.I. it had been decided that we must all practise 'freelance' interceptions. The G.C.I. Controller could cope properly with only one interception at a time, although he could put the fighter he was controlling in a most advantageous position. It was obviously wrong, however, for the other patrolling fighters just to wait until the Controller could take them over.

Co-operation with searchlights would have been one possible solution for these fighters, but most of the searchlights were way down south and there were very few left for our area. The

Sector Controller was in a position to bring a fighter to within about five miles of a bomber, and with the aid of A.I. and a slice of luck a fighter might well make contact on a bomber under this sort of control. It would be far more difficult than under G.C.I. control as the detailed information would not be available. In other words, it would be a hit-or-miss interception which the navigator would have to snap up and interpret immediately he had contact.

These practices were carried out in daylight. The pilot of the fighter would arrange as awkward an initial contact as possible for the navigator to pick up. If the navigator coped well and brought his pilot round on approximately the same course as the target, the interception would be broken off and another one set up, in order that as many initial pick-ups as possible could be achieved.

Now that crews were becoming more efficient, on all practice exercises the aircraft acting as target had instructions to take evasive action as the other aircraft made an interception. The German bombers could not be expected to fly straight and level when they were being chased so this type of practice was bound to pay dividends eventually.

Twice in March we had chases on aircraft that were possibly hostile. On the first occasion we were freelancing when I picked up a contact. We had quite a bit of trouble in getting through cloud which was pretty solid up to about eight thousand feet and had been full of snow. The consequence was that ice had started to form on the Beau and the considerable extra weight had made climbing difficult. Still, we had managed to get above the cloud and now I had a contact.

To my dismay, however, I saw that I had no pictures at all on the azimuth tube, although the elevation tube was working perfectly. I literally did not know which way to turn when the blip inevitably vanished and I had the sad task of breaking the news to Ben. When we landed it was found that both azimuth aerials had fractured, probably due to the bad icing conditions.

I had no excuse when we had a second chase later in the month. We were freelancing again when I had a contact which

I realised much too late was coming head-on towards us. Ben did get a momentary visual on an aircraft he had no time to identify; but although he whipped the Beau round in the tightest possible turn, I did not regain A.I. contact. I was furious with myself, but Ben took it very well.

The weather improved in April, but the enemy kept very quiet, at least in our area. We managed to get quite a bit of flying with the consequent practice and Ben had four sessions of air flying. By the end of the month my total flying hours were beginning to look more respectable, a hundred and forty day hours and forty-six night.

On May 1st 'B' Flight was Duty flight and Ben and I were about sixth off on the programme. Two Beaus had gone off on patrol at dusk but after an hour or so the weather had deteriorated so badly that they were recalled. In spite of the weather, Sector required all crews to remain at readiness, so out came the cards and the chess sets as we settled down for a long wait. Just before midnight the Flight Commander asked Sector if there could be any relaxation in the state of readiness – in other words, if some of us could go to bed. Sector would have none of this, however; they said that some enemy activity was expected. That put us on our toes.

The weather had improved. There was bright moonlight shining through scattered low clouds as we saw when we put our heads outside for a breath of fresh air.

An hour and a half slipped away. Although we were still on our toes, the arches of our feet were aching slightly! Suddenly the ops telephone rang. The Flight Commander leapt to it. He repeated Sector's order:

'Scramble four aircraft!'

Eight chaps, bulky in flying kit, scurried around grabbing what they needed and in seconds were shooting through the door. The call had gone to the ground crews telling them which aircraft were going off. One by one we heard the roar of engines starting up – if only Sector would ask for a couple more aircraft to scramble.

The Flight Commander had been second off on the Night

State, and Ben, as senior pilot left on the ground, was in charge He picked up the ops telephone after a few minutes and we heard him ask:

'What's the form, chum?'

Sector told him about a dozen probable Huns had been plotted heading for the Tynemouth area. Why on earth didn't they send some more Beaus off?

We waited impatiently for nearly half an hour and then a telephone rang. Our hearts leapt – then dropped through the floor when we realised that it was not the ops telephone but the ordinary station telephone. Ben answered it and we soon gathered from the tone of his voice that something out of the ordinary was going on.

The Squadron Commander, Wing Commander Heycock, was at the other end of the telephone. As was the normal practice, he had been informed that some Huns were thought to be around. He had hopped into his car, dashed from his Married Quarter down to 'A' Flight and wanted a ground crew to start his aircraft and a navigator to fly with him. At the same time he told Ben that Sector wanted two more Beaus off and he, the Wingco, would be one of the two.

Ben signalled to the next crew due off and passed the word for a ground crew to go to 'A' Flight, whilst still talking to the C.O. who then obviously asked him which navigators were left in 'B' Flight.

Ben looked around at us and reeled off our names. After a few moments' expostulation he put the telephone down disgustedly and told me to go over to 'A' Flight to fly with the C.O.

The C.O. usually flew from 'A' Flight, but, instead of always taking his turn on the programme, he had arranged that he and his navigator should be told whenever there was any activity so that they could get into the air. On this occasion the message had not reached his navigator so he had ordered Ben to send me along.

It was a bit much: not only was the C.O. grabbing Ben's place on the Night Flying Programme, but he was grabbing his navigator as well. Still, an order was an order, so off I went. It was always interesting to fly with a new pilot, but on an occasion like this I would have preferred to have been with Ben.

In a few minutes we were thundering down the runway. We lurched into the air and climbed as fast as the Beau could go. The Sector Controller gave us a vector to steer and we headed out over the coast, still climbing. When we had reached about nine thousand feet we were told to go over to Blackbird control. They informed us that there was some 'trade' about and were soon able to give me quite a good contact. I told the Wingco that I could hold it; he informed Blackbird and we went over to intercom.

My troubles were about to begin. I had noticed that my pilot was terrifically keyed up and excited. When he had been given a new course to steer by the Controller, the Beau had just about stood on one wing as the Wingco had jerked it round, instead of the standardised controlled turn I was used to with Ben.

As soon as I took over the interception and began my instructions and patter the Beau was flung all over the sky to the accompaniment of yells, curses and imprecations from the front seat. This chap was far too keen; he did not realise that he was making my job fifty times as difficult as it need be. His violent reactions to my instructions made it almost impossible for me to assess what the aircraft in front of us was doing. Every time I mentioned the word 'turn', we whipped round in a flash and the blip would jerk from one side to the other of the azimuth time base.

There was no time to remonstrate with him. As soon as the blip showed almost dead ahead I gave no more turns for a while. In the meantime, the range was closing quite well. I gave a few more turns, pleading for gentle ones and easing him out of them almost before they had begun. He became coherent long enough to reply to my query: 'Where do you want him?'

'Wherever you *blank* well like! Hurry up, man! Pull your *blank* finger out. Where is the *blank* thing?'

Luckily the *blank* thing was not far off. I managed to bring him in with the target very slightly below and to port. With the moonlight on the low cloud he got a visual at nearly two thousand five hundred feet on a Dornier 217, probably the most easy German aircraft to recognise.

The excitement at the front end of the Beau redoubled. The aircraft seemed to throw itself at the Dornier with guns blazing in a long burst. He had fired from a bit too far away, instead of stalking for a while and getting into a really good firing position. The result was no strikes, but the Dornier spotted us and became most unfriendly. It took violent evasive action, one of its gunners piping tracer bullets towards us. Tracer is always frightening at night; it seems to be coming straight at you. The trouble was that this particular tracer was actually coming straight at us. And it was hitting us.

Luckily Beau and Dornier lost sight of each other after a very short while. I still had A.I. contact, though, and we made another approach, rather more carefully this time, though the Wingco was screaming with frustration and excitement. Seconds later the Wingco saw the Dornier again. This time he got in closer and took better aim, for we saw strikes all along the fuselage. It went almost straight down in a dive, no guns firing now.

We followed it down and saw it go into cloud at a very steep angle. It was too low for our A.I. to be of use as the cloud tops were only two thousand five hundred feet, and though we watched the spot where we had last seen it we saw no flash that would denote that it had crashed.

There was nothing more doing that night, but as the clouds had gathered very low over Acklington we were diverted to Ouston, our Sector Station, where we spent the rest of the night.

When we returned to Acklington next morning I learned that Ben had eventually managed to rustle up a navigator from somewhere the night before and had been airborne. They had no joy, though.

The Wingco and I were given a probable for the Dornier.

Ben and I went to Drem for a four-day detachment on May 3rd. We carried on with the usual practices there and did some useful G.C.I. trips with our target briefed to take violent evasive action when we closed in to four thousand feet or so.

When we returned to Acklington we received the glad tidings that 141 Squadron was to re-equip with a new type of A.I. which needed a completely different aerial to Mark 4. This meant new Beaus as well, so the pilots were as pleased as the navigators.

I was detailed to attend a special course in the use of the new A.I. at the Fighter Interception Unit at Ford, in Sussex. I was to report there on May 13th, so Ben and I went off on leave, he to Edinburgh and I to London.

While I was walking in Maida Vale one day during this leave I ran into Terry Thomas. I had known him from my film days when we were both doing crowd work and small parts. We were both in uniform, he in that of an Army sergeant. I remember him saying:

'Cor, what a shower! I wish I was in your mob.'

Chapter V

MARK SEVEN

WHEN I got to Ford I found that the new A.I. was known as Mark 7. Although it worked on the same basic principle as Mark 4, the main difference was a more powerful beamed transmission which gave greater maximum range and also, to a very large extent, eliminated ground returns. The beam of the transmitter was in the shape of a cone, reaching out at forty-five degrees from the nose of the fighter each way. Both transmitting and receiving aerials were in the nose of the aircraft and were concealed in a Perspex dome attached to the front.

So far as the navigator was concerned operating looked as if it would be much easier than on Mark 4. There was only one tube for him to have to worry about; on this tube, about six inches in diameter, he was shown range, azimuth and elevation in a very simple form. Taking the centre of the tube to represent his own aircraft, the blip of a target aircraft would show as a circle, or part of a circle, of light. An aircraft dead ahead and absolutely level with the fighter would show as a complete circle, the range being assessed by the distance of the circle from the centre of the tube. If the target went slightly to one side, the circle would break, and when the target had gone out to ten degrees would show as a half-circle on that side. At fifteen degrees there would be an arc which would gradually get smaller the further the target went over. At forty degrees the arc was very small, and at forty-five degrees the target would be outside the coverage of the transmitter's cone of search.

Elevation was read in exactly the same way. Briefly, remembering that the centre of the tube represented the fighter, the position of the blip showed the exact actual position of the target relative to the fighter. Thus, if one imagined the tube to be a clockface, the target's position could be read straight off the tube to the pilot. He in turn could look upon his windscreen as a clockface, and when the navigator told him a target was two o'clock twenty degrees he would know exactly where to look for it. This method of clockface references for interception purposes became standardised soon after the introduction of Mark 7 A.I. to squadron service.

The course at Ford lasted only three days, but I managed to get in five trips which averaged just over an hour each. The practice Mark 7 was installed in Beaus just as it would be when we got our own. I was delighted with it. The only difficulty that anyone could foresee was that as a target came close to the fighter the transmitter's beam became relatively narrow, so that evasive action would have to be reacted to immediately or the target aircraft would get away. To compensate for this, however, Mark 7 did give instantaneous warning of any movement of the target.

When I returned to Acklington I found that I was to assist the Navigator Leader, who had already done the Ford course, in training the rest of 141 Squadron's navigators. He took on the training of 'A' Flight while I had a go at the 'B' Flight boys. Except for one night trip on the very last day of May, all our flying was carried out by day. We fitted a black cover inside the Perspex dome of the navigator's compartment so that the rubber visor could be taken off the indicator unit of the A.I. Two or three navigators could then gather round the tube while I explained how it worked. After two demonstrations, which included a few minutes for each navigator to operate the set, they knew enough about it to carry on by themselves.

We found it very useful and profitable to fly each of the pilots in turn as passengers, so that they could see what the navigator had to cope with during an interception. They found it all very interesting, and I am sure it was of benefit later on.

The night trip at the end of the month was of great interest.

The C.H.L., or Chain Home Low stations, were the low-level part of the general warning system. Attempts had been made to control night fighters operating at low level, two thousand feet or less, using C.H.L. information. The trouble had been that Mark 4 A.I. was unable to see so low down. Now we had A.I. that could operate at this level or even lower. Mine-laying or reconnaissance aircraft had been able to come in at this height almost at will. Now we had something with which to combat them and our first night patrol with C.H.L. showed us that it would work. We were on patrol with another Beau and carried out practice interceptions just as we normally did with G.C.I. control. We found that it all went very well but that low flying over the sea was tricky. Special altimeters were fitted to the squadron's aircraft soon after this and they proved very efficient.

The new Beau had come in fast so that by the beginning of June 141 Squadron was fully re-equipped. By dint of some pretty strenuous flying – sometimes we were up three or four times a day – the basic training of all the navigators was completed by June 3rd. There was no doubt about it, we were very pleased with our new equipment.

Early in June we heard from our pals on the Turbinlite Flight that the higher-ups had realised the futility of continuing with this cumbersome operation. Not a single success had been gained by Turbinlites. Trained crews and useful equipment were being wasted, but instead of cutting their losses and retiring the Turbinlites, gratefully and gracefully, a strange decision was made. Sector Controllers were told that the next time there was any enemy activity Turbinlites were to be given absolute priority in the use of G.C.I. control facilities.

They did not have to wait long for their last fling. On the night of June 4th, 1942, a raid of some twenty enemy aircraft was plotted coming into the Tynemouth area.

'B' Flight was on duty that night. Ben and I were some way down the night-flying programme. We knew that the Turbin-lites had been ordered off and we waited impatiently as four

Beaus, then another two, had been scrambled. We were next off. The first aircraft had gone off about half an hour after midnight. We knew that three or four Turbinlites and six Beaus were already up there. Would they want any more? We seemed to be waiting for hours; after all, this was what we had put in all those hours of training and practice for, and here we were on the ground. Fifteen long minutes had, in fact, gone before we heard the welcome ring of the ops telephone. We were off.

We must surely have broken all records in getting off and climbing up towards the east. We could see bursts of ack-ack shells over the estuary of the Tyne as we called the Sector Controller. It looked as if the raid was well and truly on; our only chance of a chase would be on something going home.

To our surprise and disgust we were told to carry on with our easterly course, away from the raid in progress. The G.C.I. Controllers would obviously have their hands full, but this seemed daft. We were flying at nearly five miles a minute, still to the east. My A.I. looked as if it was working beautifully, but we wanted something to chase. After about six minutes Ben suddenly said:

'Nuts to this. I bet the ruddy Controller is having a cup of tea and a bun. He's forgotten all about us. I'll give him a call. . . .

'Hello, Homestead. Rounder three-six. Any news? Still steering zero nine zero, angels ten.'

'Hello, three-six. Continue on zero nine zero. There should be something for you in a few minutes.'

'Zero nine zero. Listening out.'

'What do you make of that?' I asked Ben.

'Maybe there's another raid coming in. Let's hope so.'

The Hercules engines seemed to take on a more menacing roar and I could imagine Ben settling himself down in his seat. For the twentieth time since we had been airborne I made the minutest adjustments to my already perfect picture.

'Hello, Rounder three-six. Bandits in your vicinity now. Good luck.'

Mark 7 had a maximum range of about seven miles. My eyes

were straining; I was willing something to show up on the screen.

Then it was there. Maximum range, slightly starboard and about level. Switch over to intercom.

'Contact. Range seven miles, slightly starboard, about the same height.'

'Good show.'

'Range decreasing pretty fast. . . . It looks like a head-on . . . Get ready for a turn port.'

'Right.'

The range was certainly decreasing fast. It was still a bit out to starboard – we must have been on almost parallel courses – and just a bit below us.

I knew the drill for what we would have to do. The practices were paying off. Leave it over to starboard. Wait till it was about six thousand feet away and then turn away from it through a hundred and eighty degrees in a hard turn. We would have to lose a bit of height too. If we turned too soon we might finish up in front of it; too late, and we would be faced with a long stern chase. Turn towards it and we would be flying across its course and might be seen. No, our manoeuvre was to turn away from it, and if all went well we should finish up about three or four thousand feet behind, and I knew that as we nearly finished our turn I could expect to see it again on my A.I., coming in from port.

The range was nearly down to six thousand feet now.

'Hard port a hundred and eighty degrees. Go down a thousand. Let me know when you're nearly round.'

'Port a hundred and eighty degrees. Down a thousand.'

It worked like a charm; we finished up just where we should have been. We closed in without any difficulty to about two thousand feet, when Ben got his visual. From a little closer in he identified it by twin fins and thin fuselage as a Dornier 217 and I was able to turn around to look for myself.

Ben wasted no time. He closed in to four hundred feet and gave it a two-second burst. There were strikes on the tail unit and a large white flash came from the starboard engine. A burst of inaccurate return fire came from the dorsal turret. Then the Dornier turned on to its back as the port wing went under. It dropped in an almost vertical dive, with the Beau behind, too far behind for Ben to get another shot in.

We reached five thousand feet, with the Dornier screaming away from us still going down almost vertically. It drew away from us until we lost it in thick haze. The time was 01.15 a.m. and we were about fifteen miles east of the Tyne. We circled for a few minutes but did not see it go into the sea, nor could I pick it up again on A.I.

We climbed again and called Homestead to inform him of our combat and to see if there was anything else doing. We could see ack-ack bursts and a few searchlight beams over the Newcastle area. Apart from the thick low haze it was clear, although there was no moon.

Homestead told us to fly at eight thousand feet and put us on a north-south patrol some twenty miles out to sea. At about 01.30 we were warned that there was something near us but to investigate carefully as there were several friends around.

A minute or two later I had another contact, this time on an aircraft crossing us from starboard to port and slightly below us at a range of five miles. We turned quickly to port in order to cut him off, losing height as we did so. There was no difficulty in closing in on an aircraft that was weaving gently from side to side but flying level. Ben had his visual at nearly two thousand feet and I turned to watch proceedings. We had to go in to just under one thousand feet before we identified it as another Dornier 217. Our luck was certainly holding. We had really expected to see a Beau this time.

Ben gave it a two-second burst, which produced strikes all along the fuselage. It also produced some fairly accurate fire from the Dornier's turret. The tracer hosed up towards us and then swept over us. Ben gave it a second short burst, which silenced the gunner. Just as well, for in the next second Ben had to pull right up over the Dornier to avoid ramming it. The belly of the Beau would have made an excellent target for the gunner.

72

As Ben pulled the Beau up, the Dornier dropped away to port in a steep dive. We were a bit late in getting round and down after him. Although I could see him on A.I. about three miles away he was diving too steeply and I soon lost him as he drew away.

We were credited with a probable for the first combat and a damaged for the second. Again we had drawn first blood for the squadron with the new equipment and the Mark 7 A.I. had proved itself. The only weakness that had been exposed was that the navigator was at a big disadvantage when trying to follow an aircraft down in a steep dive. While his own aircraft was pointing almost straight down at the ground, his A.I. tube was apt to be swamped with ground returns which obscured the blip he was chasing.

There was always something to learn, even at this stage. Ben was kicking himself for not having polished off these two Dorniers properly. It was apparent that we must stalk our victim extremely carefully and try to get in a really punishing burst of fire without his suspecting our presence. Once a really determined enemy pilot knew he was being chased by a night fighter he could, and undoubtedly would, turn his aircraft almost inside out to escape. Even a mediocre bomber pilot would make himself very difficult to follow under these circumstances.

The raid had been a fairly big one for those days. Some thirty bombers, flying in two waves, had attacked the Newcastle area and had run into fairly stiff opposition from the guns. The Dorniers were obviously on their guard. Although the Turbinlites had monopolised the G.C.I. they had had no success, and I believe that it was the very last time they operated.

During the next few days Ben managed to get in quite a lot of air-firing practice.

In the second week in June we were to have a little light relief. Flight Lieutenant Cosby was getting married and Ben was to be best man. Koz's navigator, Pete Bowman, and I were given a couple of days off to help represent the squadron at the wedding which was to be held in London.

We had worked out a very good schedule. We would board a train to Newcastle that left nearby Ashington at about 14.00 hours on the day before the wedding. We would arrive in Newcastle at about 16.00 hours and, after a cup of tea, repair to the Turkish baths for a couple of hours. Dinner was next on the list, and then by the greatest good chance Number 13 Group Fighter Command, in which we served, was holding a Headquarters Ball at Newcastle Assembly Rooms. We had all managed to get an invitation to the ball through a W.A.A.F. Officer of Ben's acquaintance. At 22.30 hours the night train left Newcastle for London. What could be better or simpler? – that was what we thought.

At about 11 o'clock on the morning of the great day a select party was assembled in the bar of the officers' mess for a drink or two before the wedding party had lunch and set off for Newcastle. Beer was the usual aircrew drink, and it would perhaps be as well at this point to state that, although aircrew personnel were not generally noted for their abstinence, I came across very few hard drinkers in the R.A.F. Beer usually seemed to be regarded as Best. Let me say also, though, that, given the slightest excuse for a party, no better body of men existed anywhere to make the most of it.

Our little party was having a quiet beer or two, but, as more and more chaps came in after the morning's flying, the two or three beers became three or four or more. Nevertheless, all was under control until the Wingco arrived and insisted on putting a large rum into each beer. From that moment on the situation definitely deteriorated. Pete Bowman and I decided that we needed something solid inside us and we went in for lunch in a happy mood. Eventually the groom-to-be followed us but nothing could move Ben from the bar, where there appeared to be all the makings of a right royal party.

After lunch we went back to the bar for another noggin or two, until somebody suddenly realised that we would be hard put to it to catch our train, unless we pulled our fingers out. We were poured into various vehicles and a cavalcade of cars rushed us to Ashington station. We arrived three minutes after the train should have left, but, as the train was ten minutes late, all was well. An hilarious crowd of officers pushed us into a compartment and we were off. All was well for a few moments only, however, for we found that we were in a buffet car, not an ordinary compartment. True, the buffet car served only tea or coffee, but Ben produced a full bottle of whisky from somewhere with a conjurer's flourish and the position became somewhat more complicated. Pete Bowman and I decided that we could not face up to Scotch, so we found some seats and retired temporarily from action.

When we arrived at Newcastle Pete and I looked for Ben and Koz. We were just in time to see Ben disappearing arm in arm with the roughest, toughest Norwegian sailor I had ever seen. We spotted Koz, who informed us that Ben had chummed up with the matelot in the buffet car and between them they had demolished the bottle of whisky, no doubt with the aid of Koz, who was now just a little worried about his best man. Koz decided that he must go forth and find him, so we agreed to meet later on at the Assembly Rooms.

Pete and I agreed that what we needed was a good long walk, so we decided to skip the Turkish bath, had a lengthy walk around the town and finished up in an excellent grill-room. We partook of a sumptuous repast, complete with wine and liqueurs. By this time it was nearly eight o'clock. In those days of the blackout the Ball started at seven, so we ambled gently along to the Assembly Rooms.

As we mounted the stairs we heard the soft music of a dance band and the not-so-soft sound of a voice which seemed to be demanding brandy. It was quite unmistakably Ben's voice. We tracked him to an ante-room which was in use as a coffee bar. He was being told most politely that there was no brandy there, but he seemed to think they were keeping it under the counter. His eyes were slightly glazed, but he was quite steady, so we took him off to a real bar for a drink. Koz was there, looking a little the worse for wear, though he was in palpably better shape than his best man.

Koz told us that he had been hard put to it to shake off the Norwegian sailor, whom Ben had rather wanted to take to the Ball. Koz was now a trifle worried about the prospect of us all getting down to London intact for the morrow. I for one could see his point. He said that we should all 'stick together', but Ben was as slippery as quicksilver and had already vanished. We learned that he had caused something of a commotion earlier by storming into the Air Officer Commanding's private bar and demanding brandy. Luckily the A.O.C. had not been there and a friendly staff officer had attended to him.

When he was not engaged in the search for liquid refreshment Ben spent his time at the Ball looking for the W.A.A.F. officer who had kindly helped us in obtaining invitations and whom he had arranged to meet there in order to thank her. All W.A.A.F.s look pretty much alike in uniform so things were not too easy for him. He had therefore adopted the idea of tapping the shoulder of each W.A.A.F. officer that he saw, and when the face turned out to be other than the one for which he was seeking he used a formula then in current use: 'Not you, Momma. Sit down!' There were several astonished females about the place.

Eventually he managed to find the right one, and I must give her full marks. She turned out to be an angel in disguise, for she assessed the situation at once and actually managed to keep Ben out of mischief, or almost. She could not stop him from sliding a few potted palms across the ballroom floor in the middle of a dance and it was through no fault of hers that Ben tripped up the A.O.C. during a dance: that was the unfortunate sort of accident that could have happened to anyone.

By some truly remarkable chance we were all on the platform at Newcastle station some minutes before the London train was due to leave. We found an empty compartment and settled down for a comfortable journey. Ben had different thoughts about this, however. Announcing that he was going to see if he could get a drink, he had slipped through the door before anyone could move to stop him. He has long legs and used them to very good advantage, making his way along the platform, with the three of us in hot pursuit.

On his way he noticed a rather small bicycle resting unattended against some luggage. He leapt on to it and for a few magical moments he weaved among piles of luggage and waiting passengers. Soon the force of gravity was too much for him. The front wheel hit something and he dived over the handlebars, sliding along the platform for a few yards on his forehead. we dashed up and collected him. Apart from a badly grazed forehead he seemed to be all in one piece, so back to our compartment we trooped – this time keeping a very wary watch on Ben, who announced that he was chilly and put on his greatcoat, which he had placed on the luggage rack. To our astonishment he produced a full bottle of Scotch from one of its capacious pockets – 'for later on.'

The train moved off and we settled back in our seats with a good deal of relief. We were really on our way. Ben had settled in a corner and dozed off, but after about an hour the train slowed down rather jerkily and woke him up.

The train stopped, although we had thought it was non-stop to London. Ben opened a window to see what it was all about and we heard someone call out 'Doncaster!'

'Anywhere I can get a drink?' yelled Ben and, quick as a flash, the door was open and he was chasing back along the platform like a hare. Out we tumbled after him; we could just see him disappearing in the darkness when a guard warned us that this was not a proper stop and put his whistle to his lips.

The three of us scrambled aboard as the train started off again. We looked out of the window, but there was no sign of Ben. Koz wanted to pull the communication cord, but Pete and I restrained him. He was very depressed about it all and we tried to make suggestions about what he should do. I believe that we finally decided that the best thing would be to ring Doncaster station as soon as we arrived in London and have Ben put on the first available train. Unfortunately we were almost certain that he would not be in time for the ceremony. It was a tricky problem.

We were pretty gloomy when, about an hour after we had

drawn out of Doncaster station, we heard some raucous singing coming from down the corridor. To our great surprise and joy, Ben hove into sight, brandishing an almost empty bottle of whisky in one hand and with his other arm round the guard's neck. He had just managed to jump aboard into the guard's van and had enjoyed a little party with the occupant of the van before setting off in search of us.

We all duly arrived at the wedding. The graze on Ben's forehead gave him an air of bravado that went well with his uniform.

Chapter VI

LOFTY HAMER'S EPIC FLIGHT

WE returned to Acklington to receive the glad tidings that the squadron was to move to Tangmere on 23rd June. Tangmere was a really plum posting, right on the South Coast near Bognor Regis; since the beginning of the Battle of Britain it had seen lots of action. Every night flight from there had to be an operational patrol in view of the fact that the long-range warning system was not so effective against low-flying aircraft and a good deal of anti-shipping reconnaissance took place in the English Channel. A patrolling Beau would often be whizzed off to identify a plot that had suddenly popped up on the ground station's radar screen.

It was grand to be in the sunny south and 141 Squadron had the good fortune to be allotted the greater part of an exceedingly pleasant private house as a squadron mess. It was a really beautiful, large house standing in its own grounds and the owner still lived in part of it. Nearly all the original furniture had been left in the rooms, and in the lounge there was a super radiogram with stacks of excellent records. The lady of the house would bring wonderful bunches of flowers with which she would adorn the lounge. Vegetables and salads from the kitchen garden helped out the food sent to us from Tangmere which was some four miles away, and a hard tennis court and a squash court were available for our use. I cannot remember the name of the house now nor of the owner, but we were certainly lucky and very grateful.

As a matter of fact, for the remainder of my operational service with night-fighter squadrons the aircrew always had a large house some distance from the airfield for a mess. This was in order that the normal daily routine of a station mess should not disturb us if we had been flying until the early hours of the morning. The set-up was not always as pleasant as at Tangmere, but we lived in some really lovely houses. With hardly any exceptions, the chaps appreciated their good fortune and respected the property.

While we were at Tangmere preparations were in hand for the Dieppe Raid, although we did not know that at the time.

I was standing outside dispersal one day when a jeep full of chaps in R.A.F. uniform drove by. I spotted some faces I knew and waved for it to stop. They were members of the R.A.F. Film Unit, and most of them were cameramen from Denham studios where I had known them before the war. The C.O. was Teddy Baird, who had been the most popular assistant director in the film business before he left to join up in 1940. They were destined to do some grand work which included superb shots of low-level bombing raids taken under operational conditions.

The stay in the south was to be short-lived for Ben and me, however, and in exactly one month we were posted as instructors to 62 Operational Training Unit at Usworth, near Sunderland. Before we left we carried out seven patrols at Tangmere, but unfortunately we hit on a quiet spell while we were there. We had one chase after a possible Bandit but did not get near enough to establish contact on A.I. My hours of flying had risen to two hundred and two by day and eighty-two by night.

Our move to 62 Operational Training Unit was part of a new deal for the training side of Fighter Command. An appreciation of the standard of instruction at the O.T.U.s had been made when squadrons, particularly night-fighter squadrons, complained of the poor quality of new crews. The answer to the problem was very simple: the large majority of the instructors were sadly lacking in operational experience or in ability.

In the past, when instructors had been required from them, squadrons had used the request as an opportunity for getting rid of their least useful crews. Fighter Command had therefore decided that in future they would ask for instructors by name. The tour as instructor would last between six and nine months and would count as a rest from operational flying.

Ben had been on Operations far longer than I had and he was certainly due for a rest. As it was realised that teamwork played such an important part in successful night fighting, crews were sent on rest together. That was why I found myself Usworth-bound although I had been on a squadron for only a year.

Very rightly, an almost clean sweep was being made of the most experienced crews on all squadrons to ensure that they did their share of instructing, which was obviously so important if well-trained crews were to come to the squadrons from the O.T.U.s.

In the extremely sensible way in which Fighter Command usually acted, the position was explained to the crews involved. I feel it only right to say that as a member of aircrew I was always treated as an intelligent adult. I was never in the un-happy position of wondering what on earth was going on so far as my own particular relationship to the war in general was concernted. At all times we were kept up to date with developments in the main trend of the war, and through the Intelligence Section, which was an important feature of all operational R.A.F. stations, anyone who wished to keep in touch with current events was encouraged to do so. In my experience nothing was too much trouble for the often very hard-worked Intelligence officers, and the information avail-able was amazing in its scope. The whole Intelligence set-up seemed to me to be worthy of the highest praise and we were to find that this applied even more later on, when we were engaged in offensive operations.

Ben and I spent three months at Usworth, where our job was the training of navigators in the basic use of A.I. Mark 4 A.I. was used for this and we flew in Anson aircraft which had been converted into flying classrooms in which an instructor could deal with two pupils at a time. Although it was a fairly interest-ing job for me, it soon became very boring for Ben, who spent

81

most of his time flying the classrooms.

In September 1942 Ben and I were informed that we had both been awarded the D.F.C. For some while at the beginning of the war, it had been decided that personalities should be suppressed when mention was made in the Press of any specific operation. After a while it was realised that an excellent opportunity for recruiting publicity was being missed. I do not know if a similar thing was done in the other Services, but in the R.A.F. a form was sent to all aircrew in which they were asked to supply some details of their pre-Service life.

Presumably as a direct result of this some of the London papers mentioned my name and my connection with Robert Donat. I received a telegram of congratulations from Donat, followed by a letter in which he asked me to look him up next time I was in London. He was engaged in making a film, *The Adventures of Tartu*, at the old Gaumont British studios in Lime Grove, better known now as television studios. I had a forty-eight-hour pass soon after and made a point of going to see him. I spent a very pleasant afternoon at the studios and a publicity still was taken, with Donat wearing the uniform of an officer in the Roumanian Iron Guard and Brandon in his Royal Air Force uniform.

A few months later Ben and I were on leave in London whilst Donat was playing in the stage show of Shaw's *The Devil's Disciple*. We saw the play and thoroughly enjoyed it before going round to his dressing-room for a chat. He was a grand actor, and it was a great pity that so much of his acting life should have been dogged by ill health.

Although I was slightly darker and a couple of inches taller than Donat, I doubled for him several times in his films as well as being his stand-in. He usually seemed to be cast to play opposite rather tall actresses – Marlene Dietrich, Rosalind Russell and Greer Garson – so that he used to build himself up more or less to my height. With a little make-up, there really was a remarkable resemblance between us.

I doubled for him in two or three scenes during the filming of *The Ghost Goes West*, for which he wore a kilt and pencil moustache. Of course I was dressed identically to him and the make-up department had given me a moustache just like Donat's so that I was often mistaken for him. Bob was sitting just off the set one day between shots, while the final lighting adjustments for the next scene were being made with me. One of the electricians went over to him and said:

'Hello, Lew. I should think you get blooming well fed up, sitting around here all day.'

Bob Donat, playing up to him, smiled: 'You bet I do.'

A minute or two later the assistant director called out:

'Ready for you now, Mr Donat.'

As Bob passed me he commented:

'One of your fans thanks you don't have enough to do, Lew!'

Ben's promotion to Flight Lieutenant had come through when we were posted to Usworth and I became a Flying Officer in August. Although our jobs at Usworth were important and necessary, life was awfully tame after the thrills of night fighting. We stuck at it fairly well, but in mid-September, by some ruse which I have forgotten, we managed to get ourselves down to Tangmere for four days. We wangled a few Beau flights, but the only one we did at night was one that nobody else particularly wanted to do – a dawn patrol. As this entailed being up all night in order to take off at about 4.30 in the morning, no wonder nobody else was very keen. There was no activity and we were alone for the whole patrol, so that we were not able even to carry out practice interceptions. I remember being hard put to it to keep my eyes open and I was heartily glad when it was over.

One interesting trip we did during this short stay with 141 Squadron was to Castle Camps, a new station in process of construction situated near Cambridge. Flight Lieutenant Stevens, a pilot who had been sent on rest from Tangmere at the same time as Ben, had been posted to Castle Camps for his rest. A unit had been formed there to try out high-flying Mosquitos which had been fitted with special engines and pressurised cockpit. We had heard that there was a possibility that the Mosquito would be the night fighter of the future, so that it was an excellent opportunity of finding out something about the 'Wooden Wonder'.

We found that in spite of early teething troubles experienced on the Mosquitos the pilots were very favourably impressed with them. They certainly looked elegant and streamlined beside the snub-nosed, stocky Beaufighter.

At Tangmere we heard the sad news of the death of Lofty Hamer, the pilot with whom I had originally been crewed. He had been killed in action whilst on patrol a week before. The heroism displayed by this gallant N.C.O. was such that we heard that he had been recommended for a V.C., the only posthumous award that could be made. Unfortunately it was not granted, but that fact does not detract from his bravery.

The actual Combat Report made out by the Intelligence Officer with the aid of Flight Sergeant Walsh, Lofty's navigator, read as follows:

On September 8th, 1942, a Beaufighter, Pilot Warrant Officer Hamer, Navigator Flight Sergeant Walsh, was put on to a Bandit when airborne from Tangmere. At 1.40 a.m., a visual was obtained on a Heinkel III, one hundred feet above. Beau throttled and at three hundred feet opened fire when about fifteen miles south-east of St Alban's Head, height eight thousand feet. No strikes were seen from the first burst and a second long burst was given as the Beau closed in to two hundred feet. Strikes were seen all over the Heinkel, mostly on the starboard wing and the fuselage and the starboard engine burst into flame. There were several return bursts of fire, but the Beau was still below the Heinkel and was not hit. The Beau again dropped back to three hundred feet and a twelve-second burst of fire was given until the cannon ammunition was exhausted. There were flashes, mostly from the fuselage and tail unit, and the whole starboard wing caught fire. A large piece of the wing suddenly flew off and hit the Beau, swinging it to starboard. This enabled the Heinkel to get in a long burst of fire and the Beau's starboard engine burst into flames.

At the same time the navigator saw several red flashes around the pilot in the cockpit. He was certain the pilot was hit, but although he asked repeatedly: 'Are you okay?' all the pilot said was: 'You bastard.' And went in again with machine-guns blazing until all the return fire had been silenced.

By this time the flames from the Heinkel's furiously blazing starboard engine were blowing back right past the Beau and its starboard wing was flapping. A few seconds later the Heinkel went down in a streaming ball of fire into the sea. The pilot said in a strange, unnatural voice: 'He's ablaze now all right.' Then he asked for a homing. He was told he was about fifty miles south of Tangmere. The Beau was at six thousand feet, with the starboard engine still ablaze, so the navigator suggested baling out. The pilot eventually replied in the same strange voice: 'Hang on a bit. We may cope.'

He throttled the starboard engine right back and the fire died down to a spluttering glow, and made for home on the port engine. From this point the pilot was obviously labouring under great strain and Walsh had to suggest to him everything that he asked the Controller. He would not let Walsh do the transmitting nor would he allow him to come forward to open the front escape hatch. That, he said, would only knock off the speed, and he told Walsh to stay where he was.

Shortly afterwards he asked the Controller for the nearest land and was told to steer 010 degrees and that searchlights would help him. Two minutes later he was told that the nearest airfield was twelve miles east. He informed the Controller: 'At two thousand feet. Only a few minutes left.' Next the Controller said there was an airfield alight five miles west [presumably Hurn]. The pilot thought he turned west but subsequent events showed that he turned east.

He then said that he could see no lights anywhere and Walsh suggested that they should both bale out and again asked if he should open the front escape hatch, but the pilot said : 'No, we can't afford the speed. Hold on a sec, I think we can make it.'

Then he saw the north coast of the Isle of Wight and told Walsh he should bale out, so Walsh once again asked if he should open the front hatch, but his pilot said: 'No. I think I can make it.'

Suddenly the port engine, which had previously cut for a few seconds, stopped altogether. The pilot, after they had wished each other good luck, held the Beau at one thousand feet while Walsh baled out and made a good drop on to the beach near Newtown, Isle of Wight. The Beau, with no engines, then lost height so rapidly that the pilot, in his presumably wounded condition, could not possibly get out and, saying to the Controller, 'Afraid I'm finished. I'll have to go over now,' he crashed on the mainland near Lymington, Hampshire, and was killed. The Beau was a total wreck. Walsh felt that, although there was ample opportunity for them both to have taken a chance by baling out while over the sea, Hamer deliberately held on in his determination to bring the Beau back to base or over land, well knowing that by doing so he was almost certainly going to his own death.

Enemy aircraft confirmed as destroyed. Weather clear but dark. End of report.

The report speaks for itself, but I had a talk with Walsh. He told me something which throws more light on the incident. Hamer knew that Walsh was a non-swimmer. Only a few weeks before Hamer had been godfather at the christening of Walsh's child.

'Greater love hath no man than this, that a man lay down his life for his friend.'

After this short session with 141 Squadron, we returned to Usworth, where we remained until the end of October. We were then posted to 54 O.T.U. at Charterhall, in Scotland – just in time, I should imagine, to save Ben's reason. This establishment enjoyed the nickname of 'Slaughterhall' in the night-fighter world. Not undeservedly either, for the aircraft most in use there were Beaufighter 2s, with Rolls-Royce Merlin engines in place of the British Hercules. The engine factory of the Bristol Aeroplane Company had received several direct hits during a raid on Bristol and had been so badly damaged that there had been a considerable hold-up in the production of Hercules engines. Beaus were in such demand that, as a temporary measure, Merlin engines were installed in a number of Beaus. The Beau I with Hercules engines was a tough and reliable aircraft, albeit rather clumsy, but with Merlins it became just a little underpowered for its extremely heavy weight. This was without doubt the cause of many accidents.

Ben had been told at our interview with the Station Commander that he would be Flight Commander of one of the training squadrons. Charterhall was the most dispersed station I ever saw. Everything was miles from anywhere else and tons of leather must have been wasted in the interminable tramping from one place to another.

We eventually arrived at our new domain to find all the flight personnel outside the dispersal hut watching one of our Beau 2s which was coming in for a belly landing. We were told that the pilot was an instructor with a pupil crew aboard. He had been unable to get the undercarriage down. The usual drill was for the pilot to bring the aircraft down very carefully on the grass verge of the runway and it was inclined to be rather a spectacular landing. Luckily, however, the pilot in this case made an excellent job of his landing and nobody was hurt.

It was rather a shattering introduction to Charterhall and did nothing to dispel the rumours we had heard of the unreliability of the Beau 2. To be fair, though, I flew many times at Charterhall in them with Ben and with other pilots and never had a moment's anxiety. Incidentally, while we were stationed at Acklington with 141 Squadron we were at dispersal one day when word went round that one of the dreaded Beau 2s was circling the airfield. Somebody phoned Flying Control to ask what it was doing and received the information that it was on its way to Drem, where 264 Squadron was to re-equip from Defiants to Beau 2s. We watched as it made a perfect landing and taxied to the Flying Control tower, quite near us. The engines stopped and out stepped a trim little female figure of about five feet nothing. She was a ferry pilot on a routine job.

We could just imagine a repetition of this at Drem, with probably the whole squadron out on the airfield waiting for their fearsome replacements to arrive!

At Charterhall the navigators who had received their basic A.I. training in the Ansons at Usworth would be crewed with pilots in the last stage of their flying training. Occasionally more experienced pilots who had been flying in other Commands, or perhaps on day fighters in Fighter Command, came to Charterhall to learn a bit about night fighting and to find a navigator to fly with.

The aircraft used were mainly Beau 2s, with a few old Blenheims. My job was to fly, usually in the Beaus, with a pupil crew. The routine was for the pupil crew to carry out an interception on another aircraft. I would then criticise constructively and then do an interception myself, following this with another run by the pupil navigator. I found that this period as instructor, both at Usworth and at Charterhall, helped enormously to consolidate in my mind all the lessons I had learnt during my first operational tour. I had quite a bit of lecturing to do on the ground as well and I found that on the whole the job was interesting – but it was dull compared to operational flying. The only sensible thing to do, anyhow, was to make the best of it and we were soon able to count the days towards our return to operational flying.

Two things remain in my mind from the routine of Charterhall. Flight Lieutenant Richard Hillary, the author of that fine book *The Last Enemy*, was killed there whilst flying as a pupil. He had been shot down in flames during the Battle of Britain and had been terribly burnt. I lived in the same mess as Hillary for over two months and to me, as to several other instructors there, it seemed inevitable that he would crash eventually. His physical disabilities caused by the terrible burns he had received were such that he was not really capable of flying an operational aircraft. Somewhere along the line somebody was guilty of not accepting the responsibility for telling him what he must have known in his own heart: that he must accept the fact that his operational days were over. As it was, not only was he killed but the navigator with whom he had been crewed lost his life unnecessarily.

The other memorable event at Charterhall was the screening of the film *Pimpernel Smith*, in which I appeared as a Gestapo officer. As Charterhall was in a fairly remote spot, films were shown weekly in the various messes, and it can be imagined that my appearance on the silver screen was the cause of much comment and commotion.

Almost six months to the day after we had begun our rest Fighter Command enquired if we had any special preference for the squadron we would join for our second tour. Quite understandably we had discussed this subject many times during the past few months and we had narrowed the choice down to four squadrons. Without being conceited, we knew that any squadron was always glad to receive experienced second-tour crews, so that we would most likely be posted to the squadron which we made our first choice.

There was, of course, a sentimental hankering after 141 Squadron, which had moved from Tangmere to nearby Ford. Nearly all the chaps we had known had been posted from the squadron by now, however, and they were still equipped with Beaus.

The next two squadrons we considered were 29 and 85 Squadrons. 29 Squadron were at West Malling in Kent; although still equipped with Beaus, they were high on the priority list for Mosquitos. 85 Squadron were at Hunsdon, in Hertfordshire; they had just re-equipped with Mosquitos. Both these squadrons had been very successful in the past and not unnaturally were rather favoured by Fighter Command when any new equipment came along. They always seemed to be kept on airfields well in the forefront of operations and were certainly regarded as the plum squadrons to get to.

Finally there was 157 Squadron, almost a brand-new squadron; it had been formed in December 1941, and declared operational by the end of April 1942. It was the first night-fighter squadron to be equipped with Mosquitos, and although there had been many trials and tribulations with the Mosquitos at first, these had all been sorted out and everyone seemed to think that the Mosquito was a really fine aircraft. 157 Squadron were at Castle Camps, near Cambridge.

We decided to ask for a posting to 157 Squadron, with 29 as second choice. The main reason was that we thought that being on a fairly new squadron, with its traditions yet to be made, would give us more scope. It was a decision we never regretted.

At last the great day dawned. On February 16th, 1943, we were posted to 157 Squadron at Castle Camps. We had managed to escape after seven months as instructors. The squadron was a very happy one with a grand bunch of fellows led by a really superb Commanding Officer. Wing Commander V .J. Wheeler had won the M.C. and Bar in the First World War and had already won the D.F.C. in this war. Between wars he had been a commercial air-line pilot and had thousands of flying hours to his credit. Nobody knew his age, but we referred to him affectionately as 'Pop', though not in his hearing.

Ben had met Pop Wheeler before and had an amusing story to tell about him. While Ben was at Gravesend with 141 Squadron they were joined by 85 Squadron. This squadron had a fine record flying Hurricanes over Dunkirk and they were commanded by Peter Townsend. Townsend was furiously engaged in building up his own and the squadron's night-flying experience. He himself had about twenty or thirty night hours under war conditions, which was pretty good for those days.

One day in the bar at Gravesend a grey-haired gentleman in the uniform of a Pilot Officer reported to Townsend, saying that he had been posted to 85 Squadron and that his name was Wheeler.

90

'Good show. Have you done much night flying?' asked Townsend.

'About three thousand hours, sir,' was the reply.

'No. I meant how many night-flying hours have you done?'

'That's right, sir. About three thousand night-flying hours.'

It transpired that Pop Wheeler had some fifteen thousand hours total flying to his credit with Imperial Airways!

A great deal has been written about those 'Wooden Wonders,' the ubiquitous Mosquitos – Mozzies as they were known by those who flew in them. Originally designed as a high-level, high-speed photographic reconnaissance aircraft, it had been adapted as night fighter, light bomber, long-range day fighter and eventually it was almost doing the job of a heavy bomber. Undoubtedly the most useful and successful aircraft produced by any nation during the last war, it carried out all its roles perfectly.

In the night-fighter version the pilot and navigator sat side by side in a reasonably roomy cockpit, with the navigator to the right of the pilot and slightly behind him. This time the A.I. had been installed in such a manner that the navigator faced forward. This was altogether a much friendlier arrangement than in the Beau, as well as being more practical for the teamwork which was such an essential part of night fighting. The Mozzie was manoeuvrable, comfortable, reliable and proved to be readily adaptable for the various modifications that became necessary as more and more demands were made upon it.

The cockpit lay-out was excellent, although perhaps a trifle cramped when both members of the crew were above average size as were Ben and I. Entry and exit were effected through a small door on the right-hand side of the cockpit, and a collapsible steel ladder was carried inside, as the door was some eight feet from the ground when the Mozzie was stationary.

The A.I.-equipped fighter was armed with four 20-mm. cannons which were belt fed. Their muzzles were just under the nose of the aircraft. The long-range fighter, which did not carry A.I., carried four machine-guns as well.

Although the Mozzie was introduced into squadron service as a night fighter as early as 1942, and in spite of the immense and rapid developments in aircraft production on both sides during the next few years, it was still the best night fighter in use anywhere when the war ended three years later. It was a truly remarkable achievement by the de Havilland Aircraft Company, who had produced the Mozzie as a private venture, and by all those who helped in fitting out the night-fighter version of this amazing aircraft.

There was one snag, however. Fighter Command had perpetrated a blunder almost as bad as the Turbinlite fiasco. They had decided to install in our beautiful Mozzies, in fact in all the first batch of Mozzies to reach squadrons, a wretched new Mark of A.I. This was Mark 5 A.I., which had all the faults of the early Mark 4 plus many of its own. It was a retrograde step even when compared with Mark 4, but when compared with Mark 7 it was rather like going back to a divining-rod. There were times in the next few months when I thought that if I took a hazel twig, persuaded a Dachshund to lift a leg against it and then took the twig into the Mozzie with me, it would lead me to a German more readily than would Mark 5 A.I.

It had been wished on to Fighter Command by the experts of the Fighter Interception Unit. while it might have been all very well for these highly skilled pilots, it was not very practical for the average squadron pilot. It had the same aerial system as Mark 4 and the main difference was that it had an extra tube, placed so that the pilot could see it and could carry out the final stages of the interception himself. All the navigator needed to do was to read out the range. At night the pilot had his hands full enough without giving him an extra tube to look at. Then, too, when he should have been searching the sky for a visual, he would have to look at this indicator tube. Apart from these points, the equipment suffered from very serious limitations that were not discovered until we had been struggling with it for several months.

I was so delighted to be back on a squadron that I tried not to let the drawbacks of Mark 5 get me down. We just had to make it work. Nevertheless it was really frustrating that, just when I had begun to think that I had acquired some glimmerings of knowledge regarding A.I. technique, I should begin to lose contacts that I well knew I could have held easily with Mark 7 or even Mark 4 A.I. What was even worse was that in March, on two operational patrols, I was given contacts by the G.C.I. Controllers that I failed to turn into visuals. These may or may not have been enemy planes, but it made me feel that I was letting the side down. This dislike of Mark 5 was by no means confined to navigators or even to 157 Squadron. Command were told of this dislike very forcibly by all squadrons, but unfortunately a large number of sets had been made and it took some time to get them replaced.

Consolation was just around the corner, however, for the night-fighter force had become so formidable in comparison with the greatly reduced enemy activity that it was decided to turn some of its strength to offensive operations. At this stage of the war there were some twenty or more British night-fighter squadrons, each with twenty-four or more crews straining at the leash. To initiate this new spirit of offence, half a dozen crews were selected from each of eight squadrons for training, Ben and I being among those selected from 157 Squadron. An experienced crew from one of Fighter Command's Intruder squadrons was attached to us for this training which consisted of a few lectures and a short programme of cross-country navigation exercises for us to carry out.

Chapter VII

THE OFFENSIVE

As far back as the summer of 1940 a few British fighters had been allowed to prowl about at night near enemy airfields hoping to catch bombers taking off or landing. It was realised that in order to obtain the maximum possible success against a bomber raid the bombers should be attacked for as much of their journey to and from the target as possible. What better place could there be for our fighters to start and finish than the enemy's airfields?

For a while this operation, which had become known as Intruder, had been carried out by a few selected pilots from the night-fighter squadrons, with the odd Hurricane or two operating on bright moonlight nights. These 'cat's-eye' aircraft – that is to say, aircraft operating by night but not carrying A.I. – had enjoyed considerable success and two or three Intruder squadrons had been formed. These squadrons flew Havocs at first, but they were replaced by Mozzies, which proved admirable aircraft for the job.

As these specialist Intruder squadrons became experienced, they operated in all conditions of darkness, not relying on bright moonlight to aid them in navigation or seeing their potential victims. They were not allowed to carry A.I., however, because of the danger of an Intruder being shot down over enemy territory. The German radar experts might have been able to learn too much from our A.I., if they had been able to gather the parts from a wrecked aircraft, and use it against our bombers.

In spite of the fact that no A.I. was carried, the Intruders managed to shoot down a considerable number of German planes. If an enemy bomber raid was expected, Intruders would take off to patrol as many known German bomber bases as possible. They would try to arrive just at the time when the bombers were taking off; and, of course, if they saw a bomber taking off, they did not have to worry about identifying it. A second wave of Intruders would take off so as to be on patrol near enemy airfields when the bombers were trying to land. If visibility was good enough they would also shoot up aircraft parked on the airfield – an extremely difficult and dangerous operation this, but one in which they soon excelled.

Undoubtedly one of the reasons for their success in destroying so many enemy aircraft by night was that the Germans had poor night-flying training. They seemed to need lots of lights on the airfield and even kept their own navigation lights on for taxying and take-off. Ben and I were to see this for ourselves later.

In spite of the incredible successes of our Intruders, which must have been only too apparent to the Huns, they hardly reciprocated at all. Herr Hermann Goering's fatuous statement that not one bomb would fall on German soil had a very fortunate sequel. When Bomber Command began dropping bombs in ever-increasing numbers on the Reich, an order went out that all the Luftwaffe's fighters were to be used, as far as possible, for the defence of the Fatherland.

As a direct result of this, except for one brief spell which was too little and too late, Bomber Command of the R.A.F. had no trouble from German Intruders. The imagination boggles at the chaos and confusion that could have been caused by a couple of squadrons of really intrepid German Intruders when the tremendous Bomber Command raids were assembling over England. Often at a particular time hundreds of American bombers and escorting fighters would be returning from daylight raids; the skies over the North Sea and Britain would be swarming with our aircraft and ace German crews would surely have been counting their scores in dozens.

Even if Intruding had not resulted in the direct destruction of a large number of enemy aircraft, the effect on the morale of the German bomber force must have been very great. If an Intruder is thought to be in the vicinity of an airfield when bombers are taking off or landing, lights must be reduced to a minimum and the chances of a taxying or flying accident are increased. A couple of bombs, even the small ones that Intruders carried, are not calculated to ease the nerves of the bomber crews although no material damage might be done. A bomber shot down on or near its own base, either before or after a raid, is far more of a morale-destroyer than an aircraft 'missing' after a raid. It must become very wearing to be a frequent pall-bearer at the military funerals of one's erstwhile comrades.

Ben and I were very pleased to have been selected for Intruder training although I was rather worried at first by my sad lack of navigational experience. Although I was wearing the 'N' brevet, I had not done a navigation course. I found that low-level navigation was, luckily, fairly easy if one could use a little maths and a lot of common-sense, had an accurate forecast of wind and at the same time kept a sense of proportion.

The help given by Flight Lieutenant Hodder, the navigator member of the Intruder crew attached to us, was invaluable. A short navigation course had been incorporated in Ben's pilot training, so that he knew far more than I did about the job I would have to master.

Our first practice cross-country was carried out in daylight on March 20th, 1943. My log book says: *Cross-country 1a O.K.*, but I seem to remember Ben pointing out several errors that were creeping in, just in time for me to extricate myself. On all these navigation training flights Ben's patience and help was absolutely unbounded. He certainly helped me over the jittery period of my navigation. After our first cross-country we had a spell of bad weather, and I note that at 09.30 one anything-but-fine morning, we did a bad weather patrol, without any excitement other than that of getting down again all in one piece.

In April we carried out six cross-countries by day and two by night. Five of these were moderately successful, but even in my log book I could record the other three trips as only *partially successful*. Fortunately, the final night trip that we tried went as smoothly as silk; honour was saved.

157 Squadron was moved to Bradwell Bay, in Essex, in early April and so part of our training was carried out from there. Bradwell was right on the coast not far from Southend-on-Sea. It was a wonderful station from the operational point of view, with every facility one could wish for. The officers' mess had been the residence of the local M.P., Mr Tom Driberg, and very pleasant it was too.

In the very early hours of April 15th we were scrambled with several other Mozzies to intercept a raid heading for London. The Combat Report made out by the Intelligence Officer read:

Flight Lieutenant Benson reports: We took off from Bradwell at 00.15 hours on 15th April 1943, and under Debden Sector control we got A.I. contact at range of nine-thousand feet, our height ten-thousand feet, on an aircraft coming head-on towards us, and had a visual immediately afterwards. It was above us and I identified it as a Dornier from its plan view.

We did a hard turn port and saw it again, flying in and out of cloud. E/A [enemy aircraft] started fairly violent weaves and changes in height as we were closing in fast at about two hundred and seventy knots indicated air speed. We overshot and last saw E/A below and to port. A.I. contact was also lost. E/A's course was west when we picked him up over the coast south of Bradwell and he was going east when we lost him.

We were vectored back on to course 100 degrees and handed over to G.C.I. Trimley Heath, Controller Squadron Leader Kidd, who told us to stay on this vector. Contact was obtained immediately at range of ten thousand feet on an aircraft dead ahead and crossing from starboard to port. We did a hard turn and dived, as the aircraft was one thousand feet below. A visual was obtained at a range of two thousand feet, and as we came in E/A was a little above, weaving gently and changing height. We closed in rapidly and identified aircraft as a Dornier 217.

At two hundred yards I gave him a three-second burst with four cannons from astern and above, but saw no results. I fired a seven-second burst and saw strikes, first to the port engine and mainplane which immediately burst into flames. These spread down the port side of the fuselage until the whole aircraft, including the tail, was ablaze. There was no return fire. E/A went down in a shallow dive, turning to port, and finally hit the ground at 00.45 hours.

The R/T and intercom packed up when I fired and I was therefore unable to continue the patrol.

Immediately after the combat, my navigator, while changing fuses, saw another Dornier crossing behind us from port to starboard, but was unable to inform me about it in time to do anything. It was subsequently found that the ten-pin plug on the intercom amplifier had vibrated slightly out of its socket and was not making proper contact. Camera gun not used.

The wreckage of a Dornier 217 [believed to be Mk J1.] was subsequently inspected at Layer Breton Heath, Essex, and numerous 20-mm. cannons strikes were found in and around the port engine and propeller. Three of the crew baled out and were captured and the body of the Wireless Operator was found in the wreckage.

End of Report.

We had actually managed to destroy a Hun using the dreaded Mark 5 A.I., but by the same token, we had lost one that we should have destroyed. Then came the misfortune with R/T and intercom, which meant that we could not speak to the ground or to each other.

As soon as our earphones went dead I assumed that a fuse had blown. I manoeuvred round in my seat to change fuses – no easy feat in a Mozzie for someone of my bulk. The Dornier was still on its way down, flaming like a rocket. I was keeping half an eye on it as Ben banked our Mozzie to watch the inevitable crash. Between looking at the Dornier and the fusebox I suddenly caught sight of the third Dornier crossing behind us only about one thousand five hundred feet away and slightly above us. Just at that moment the crash came below us. For a second or two Ben must have thought I was banging him on the back in congratulation at our success. By the time I could make him realise, by dint of much shouting over the noise of the engines, that there was another Dornier around, it was too late to do anything about it. We had no method of communication to each other, although I was able to steer him home by sign language.

The loss of our R/T caused another incident. Our combat had taken place just north of Bradwell and had been watched by many of the station personnel. They had heard the roaring engines and the cannon fire followed by an aircraft going down in flames. The Sector Controller had told them by telephone that we were after a Hun near the airfield and so, of course, they went out to watch. Later, when the G.C.I. Controller reported that he had put us in contact with a Bandit but could no longer get any reply from us to his repeated calls on R/T, they could only assume that we had gone down in flames. Not long afterwards Ben and I landed and two very substantial ghosts walked into the crew room.

Next day we were able to drive over to see the wreckage. The Dornier had crashed quite near to a farmhouse, the only building within miles. We had noticed that it had gone into a shallow dive, and after hitting the ground had slithered along, shedding pieces all the way, and finally had come to rest some fifty yards short of the house. One wheel, all ablaze, had actually bounced over the house and had finished up in the fork of a large tree. The farmer did not seem to realise how lucky he had been that the bomber had not crashed right on his house. He was most irate because some saplings in an orchard had been badly bent!

We heard that the ack-ack guns had also claimed to have shot down our Dornier, but the cannon shells in the wreckage disproved their claim. Incidentally, we had seen no gunfire other than our own.

The next day we carried out our final cross-country trip. It was by daylight and included making a landfall on the Isle of Man. According to my navigation, the Isle of Man was still in the right place.

It had been decided by Fighter Command that we should operate only on bright moonlight nights until we became more experienced in our new role. An operation called Ranger had been devised which entailed flights over pre-planned routes into enemy territory. The targets were trains, lorries, barges and anything else that moved at night. In view of the curfew imposed by the Germans on occupied countries, these could be safely assumed to be enemy targets. If by chance we did see an enemy aircraft we were at liberty to attack.

With the willing aid of the Intelligence section Ben and I had worked out half a dozen sorties. These had been registered with Fighter Command so that on the first suitable night we would be able to select the most likely-looking one. Intelligence would pass on our actual times of crossing out and returning so that we would not be mistaken for enemy raiders.

We did not have to wait very long, for three days later conditions were just right for our first trip over enemy territory. Our plan was to cross out at Beachy Head, enter France near Le Treport, on past Lens and Cambrai to St Quentin, from which a very busy railway line led to Paris. We would patrol this line between St Quentin and Creil, about twenty miles from Paris. This line was used quite a bit by Germans going to and from leave in Paris. We hoped to assist in making at least part of their leave memorable.

I do not know how Ben was feeling about this first offensive sortie, but, although I was terrifically keen to have a go, I fully expected that the moment we crossed the enemy coast we would be continuously bathed in searchlights, fired at from the ground with every sort of shot and shell and probably chased by fighters into the bargain. I really believe, however, that I was rather more worried by my lack of navigational skill than by anything else, such was my faith in Ben, the Mozzie and my good luck.

We tested our Mozzie that afternoon. We were to fly a long-range day-fighter version in view of the fact that we could not take A.I. over enemy territory. All went well and we then had a long wait, as the right conditions of moonlight would not occur until almost midnight; we were due off an hour before midnight. There was a final Intelligence check-up and Met. forecast, then we were on our way to the aircraft.

Ben taxied to the end of the runway, and as he opened up the engines for take off said exultantly:

'Well, chaps, here we go!'

We climbed on course for Beachy Head, and after a few minutes, when we were crossing the Thames Estuary near Tilbury, some bright spark began firing at us from the ground. He was way behind us with his aim, but I hurriedly flashed a recognition signal and the firing ceased. Everyone should have been briefed about our trip, so someone had blundered.

It was a glorious night and we could see the moon coming up as we passed over Beachy Head. At the same time, I took a quick look around the cockpit to see that everything was in order. I noticed that the voltmeter was reading low and called Ben's attention to it.

'Hey, Ben! The voltmeter is reading twenty-four volts. It's usually about twenty-seven or twenty-eight.'

'Well, everything seems to be working all right.'

'Yes. It's probably only the Mozzies fitted with A.I. where it has to be twenty-seven volts or more for the stuff to work properly.'

'Good enough. Now we've got this far on the perishing trip I don't want to turn round.'

'I quite agree. Let's press on.'

Press on we did. Low and fast over the sea, we had been told, so low and fast it was. At five hundred feet their radar would not get much warning of our approach. The sea crossing did not take very long – about twenty minutes. Then we were approaching the enemy coast. Climbed a bit as we neared the coast, then up to three thousand feet as we went over to give us more room in which to manoeuvre if we were engaged by guns or searchlights. Meanwhile I had to look for the vital landfall which would tell me if we were on course.

Good – we had hit the coast dead on track. I gave Ben the course to steer for Lens. Nobody seemed to be taking any notice of us as we made our way to our stretch of railway, flying now at two thousand feet. My navigation was working out well. Landmarks kept showing just in the right places and the moon was shining brightly. But not a sign did we see of the wily Hun. Not a lorry, not a barge, not a train, not an aircraft, not a searchlight nor a trace of flak. It was just like a training trip.

We reached St Quentin without incident, saw our railway and turned on to our new course along towards Creil. We were down to a thousand feet now. Within a couple of minutes we saw a train puffing merrily along in the same direction as us, its smoke looking like a blob of cotton-wool in the moonlight. Ben made a wide sweep to get into a good firing position.

As he did so I pointed out a second train about a mile from the first, coming towards it. We seemed to poise for a second as Ben came out of the turn, perfectly positioned for the attack. This was the moment we had been waiting for.

Down swooped the Mozzie, straight for the engine of the first train. It looked like a toy engine as we started our dive, but it rapidly became larger until at about four hundred yards' range Ben pressed the gun button. The four cannons and four machine-guns blazed away, bringing bright flashes from the engine as the shell struck home. It was only a two-second burst though and I had expected Ben to go on blazing away until the very last moment. Then I realised that, at the very moment that the guns had stopped firing, the cockpit lighting had gone out and the R/T had a dead sound.

The aircraft was still flying well enough. We had passed over the train, climbing away from it now. The train still puffed along, perhaps not quite so merrily and with steam coming in dense clouds from places from which no steam really ought to come.

Ben switched over to intercom. To our relief we found that we could speak to one another, albeit rather faintly.

'Looks like the main fuse,' I informed Ben. 'I'll have a go at changing it.'

This was a major operation for a large navigator in the confined space of the Mozzie cockpit. For the next ten minutes or so I fiddled with fuses, but they all seemed to be in order. In the meantime Ben had muttered something about:

'Getting the hell out of here' – an idea that had my full support.

I had been astonished throughout the trip by the lack of hostility from the foe. I fully expected, particularly now that we had fired our guns in anger, to find every gun, searchlight and fighter within a couple of hundred miles after us.

After some time I decided that I was wasting my time with the fuses, so I turned around and left them alone. At this moment I noticed that the generator voltmeter was showing only eight volts. This meant that the generator was not charging the batteries and was something I could do nothing about. Clot that I was – I should have remembered about that voltmeter and not wasted time changing perfectly good fuses.

Presumably Ben had had the same ideas of imminent enemy action that had flashed through my brain. He had been taking violent evasive action in all directions at some three hundred miles an hour, although, as it happened, nobody seemed to be paying the slightest bit of attention to us.

Suddenly it dawned upon me that in all the excitement I had completely forgotten to keep my log up to date. The last entry was our arrival at St Quentin which I had been writing in when the train was spotted. Consequently I had omitted to enter the time of our arrival. Although I knew where we had attacked the train, I had little idea when the attack had taken place and still less of how long we had been taking evasive action.

When I asked Ben on what course had he been flying since the encounter, I was even more worried; he told me that he had just beetled off from the scene of the attack and really had no idea. Roughly south-east perhaps and would I give him a course to steer for home.

This set me back for a moment, then I realised that the finer points of navigation must be forgotten – I must aim for England. I gave him a course of 310 degrees to steer and fondly hoped that we might arrive in the neighbourhood of the Somme Estuary, where we had originally intended to come out.

The moon was going down and a slight haze was forming. We climbed to two thousand five hundred feet hoping to see some landmark that would assure us that we were on track. We pressed on without incident and I even went so far as to give an E.T.A. – estimated time of arrival – at the coast, which I opined we would cross in about twenty minutes.

My estimated twenty minutes joined the limbo of things lost; another ten minutes joined them. I began to feel that all was not well. A rumour was then current that the wily Hun had some sort of ray that could magnetise an area of the heavens and put the kibosh on all compasses in that area. Perhaps our compass had been affected and we had been flying south all this time – visions of a prisoner-of-war camp flashed through my mind. I passed my thoughts on to Ben, who had the presence of mind to line up our compass with the North Star. It was working very well.

Just as I was wondering if it ever would appear, we saw the coastline ahead of us. At least, we thought we did. Then we found ourselves flying slap over the middle of a large town that spread over both sides of a wide river. One of the things we had been warned against was flying near large towns. It was sheer suicide, we had been told. Nobody took the slightest notice of us and I was able at last to identify our position. We were over Le Havre, some sixty miles south-west of where I had fondly imagined we were. I gave Ben a course to steer, and as we crossed the coast, heading for Beachy Head, two search-lights lazily flicked on to us and then flicked off again. This was the only hostile act the Hun committed against us that night.

Our worries were not quite at an end, however. It was very likely that we would be plotted by our own defences as a hostile aircraft. Admittedly, we would be crossing in at Beachy Head, where we were supposed to, but we were well over half an hour late. Nor did we have any R/T with which to make contact. We did have a Very pistol, though, with the appropriate signal cartridges, and if we had been fired on by our own side that would have been a means of identification.

No one took any notice of us, though, as we flew low over the Channel to make our landfall at Beachy Head. We flew over that very welcome landmark and made our way back to base, where we ate a not-very-well-deserved night-flying supper of bacon and eggs. On this, our first trip over enemy territory, we seemed to have made every sort of boob possible – and had got away with it. One thing was certain, though: we made none of those errors on any subsequent trip.

Three nights later we carried out a second Ranger patrol, looking for barges on a network of canals. As a navigational exercise it went perfectly, but, although the moonlight was bright, there was fairly thick haze. We saw nothing to shoot at and nobody took the slightest notice of our activities so far as we knew.

Whilst the moonlight period lasted the squadron was interspersing Ranger operations with normal defensive patrols. Ben and I did our share of both, though the defensive patrols seemed to have lost some of their thrill.

Chapter VIII

THAT WAS A CHURCH STEEPLE

ON May 18th we took off just before midnight for an extensive tour of French and Belgian railways without having to worry about buying any tickets. We crossed the French coast near Dunkirk and flew to Amiens. From there we patrolled a long stretch of rail as far as Rheims without spotting anything, so we turned back along the same line with the intention of following it to St Quentin, then to Mons and home via Ostend.

We were approaching the little town of Laon, when we saw the smoke of a train ahead of us. Ben manoeuvred our Mozzie so as to have a shot at the engine with the moon behind it. I was not going to be caught out this time. As we were turning I scribbled away madly, keeping my log up to date. I looked up again just as we were coming into firing range. Suddenly something big and black whizzed past my side of the cockpit.

'What the devil was that?' I gasped.

'Oh,' said Ben, 'a church steeple. We are flying down the side of a hill.'

So we were.

The train was standing in a little station. Ben gave the engine a good burst of cannons and machine-guns and we wheeled around on to our original course again. We saw several strikes and flashes from the engine and a great cloud of steam was coming from it when we left.

At Haumont, near Mons, we saw a number of trucks in a railway siding. Two attacks on them produced good results.

We then went home without further incident, rather impressed with the knowledge that a single aircraft seemed to be able to roam around over enemy territory without much interference.

Two nights later we were on the night-flying programme for a defensive patrol. We had carried out the usual test run on our aircraft, which we had found perfectly serviceable, and it was late afternoon when we landed; we left our parachutes and flying helmets ready in the aircraft while we went off for tea.

There was no enemy activity that night, but after waiting round a while we were ordered off for a practice G.C.I. with another Mozzie. We walked out to our aircraft, struggled in and settled down. Ben signalled to the ground crew, pressed a button and one engine roared into life. A moment later he signalled again, pressed the button, but the second engine could only raise a splutter.

Several more attempts to start the engine failed. A spare aircraft which had been tested was always available, so we transferred ourselves and our kit rapidly to this other Mozzie. Both engines started promptly this time and off we went, climbing up to eighteen thousand feet for some practice runs. We acted as fighter for the first run, which went reasonably well, but towards the end of the interception I began to feel 'proper poorly'. My stomach was hurting and I could feel a headache coming on which, as I was normally very fit, was most unusual.

We became target for a while so that I had more time to feel sorry for myself. My stomach was really hurting badly now and my head aching so that my thoughts were becoming rather fuzzy. In spite of this it did occur to me that Ben was having some difficulty in understanding what the Controller was telling him. Some of the replies he was giving seemed rather puzzling although I could not put my finger on what was wrong.

A thought oozed into my fuddled mind. Oxygen! Was the oxygen switched on? Early in my flying training, lectures had been given about the danger of lack of oxygen when flying high. It could produce very strange results, the most frequent being a sense of irresponsibility and even symptoms of drunkenness.

I checked the dial that indicated the oxygen pressure. That was right, I had not forgotten to switch it on, for it was reading twenty thousand feet. As I turned my head from looking at the dial I felt something dangling from my helmet. It was my oxygen tube. In my hurry to get in to the spare Mozzie, although I had remembered to switch the oxygen on, I had omitted to plug in my tube. We had been warned to use oxygen from take-off at night and we had been airborne over an hour. I remedied my omission at once, turned the pressure to full on for a few seconds and breathed deeply. I felt much better at once.

I glanced over at Ben; sure enough, his oxygen tube was dangling from his helmet. He plugged in and we were both okay. This spot of clottishness might well have had serious consequences.

We had another uneventful Ranger trip next night, when we were again in the St Quentin area. Very thick haze made visibility extremely poor on this occasion, but it was a good navigational exercise. Two nights later, in our defensive role, we were scrambled after some Bogeys at 2.50 in the morning. The Bogeys turned out to be our own returning bombers.

On May 27th we were informed that we could consider ourselves fully operational for Intruder patrols and found that we were detailed forthwith for such a patrol that very night. We were to carry out a thirty-minute low-level Intruder patrol of Bergen/Alkmaar airfield. This was in northern Holland, about five miles inland from the North Sea, and was believed to be used by German bombers.

We took off just before midnight and made the long North Sea crossing at about four hundred feet, aiming to cross the Dutch coast some eight miles north of Bergen. As we approached the coastline we made height to two thousand five hundred feet in order to get a good view of our landfall and to have a bit of height for emergencies. We found that we were almost fifteen miles south of where we should have been. For once the wind forecast that I had been given was badly out. Instead of fifteen knots northerly it was nearer thirty knots.

Fortunately there was a large lake just inland from where we had hit the coast, so that we were able to pinpoint our position. We had agreed on a figure-of-eight patrol about five miles to the north of the airfield. The idea of flying a figure of eight was that the patrolling fighter should at all times be able to see the target and be able to dart in quickly if necessary.

We flew past the airfield, keeping fairly well over to the east, and took up our patrol. As we had passed by we had seen a few lights on the ground but it did not look very active. We were staying about five miles north, where we would be least likely to deter any intrepid enemy aviators from taking off.

It was quite a dark night with a fair amount of haze, which thickened noticeably as we patrolled. We were at two thousand feet now and the wind tended to take us towards our target. After about twenty minutes, the lights on Bergen/Alkmaar had been obscured by the haze and we were finding it increasingly difficult to see any landmarks at all. Still, we decided to stick it out for the full half-hour.

By the time our patrol was due to finish, we had climbed to five-thousand feet in the hope of seeing something through the ever-increasing murk below but without success. When we decided to call it a night, we dived for the coast on our way home. We thought we were still eight miles or so to the north of the airfield. But no – we must have drifted right over the wretched place. Suddenly the air around us was alive with tracer shells hosing their way up towards us. Our bit of extra height stood us in good stead, as Ben stuffed the nose of the Mozzie down and we gradually left the firework display behind us. It is frightening stuff, tracer at night.

We had a very interesting change of jobs in June. Ben and I were sent, with two other crews from 157 Squadron, to Predannack, in Cornwall. There we found ourselves under the orders of Coastal Command. We learned of an intriguing situation that had arisen.

The anti-U-boat warfare was mounting to a crescendo at this

109

time. Packs of U-boats were hunting out in the Atlantic, often guided by German long-range aircraft operating from western France. To combat the U-boat packs, Coastal Command had Sunderlands, Halifaxes and Liberators operating from Cornwall, flying out over the Atlantic to spot them. They had been having a fair amount of success, so much so that the Jerries had popped a squadron or two of Junkers 88s on the Brest Peninsula to chase Coastal Command's big boys. They, in turn, had asked Fighter Command to lend some Mozzies to harry the Junkers 88s. That was us.

The next move was for some Focke Wulf 190s to arrive at Brest and Mustangs in Cornwall to oppose them. So we had our own little war in the south-west.

Six night-fighter squadrons had each been told to supply three Mozzies complete with ground and air crews, making a composite squadron of eighteen aircraft. These were divided into two flights and Ben was put in command of one of these flights. When we arrived at Predannack almost the whole of Cornwall was covered in a sea mist which persisted for nearly a week and prevented any flying. With the aid of some of the Coastal chaps it gave us an opportunity of finding out something of our new role and working out some tactics.

Our job was to act as long-range day fighters for patrols in the Bay of Biscay and we were to be put to any use that Coastal Command needed us for. Our first patrol was in search of a U-boat that had been reported damaged and surfaced way out in the Bay. We took off at 10.30 on the morning of 11th June as one of a formation of six Mozzies. Straight out over the Atlantic we flew for four hundred miles.

We had been advised to fly at about a hundred feet for two reasons: we would be difficult for a vessel to see and any other aircraft about were likely to be higher than a hundred feet and would therefore be fairly easy for us to spot. Although we were to try to locate the U-boat, we had to be prepared for anything. We reached the end of our easterly leg and turned south for a hundred miles. It was a lovely summer day, with not a cloud in the sky. Our six aircraft were well spread out but there was nothing to see.

We turned for home, and when we were rather more than fifty miles from the French coast we spotted a lone trawler. We had been told that the Germans were using trawlers to pass on information to their long-range aircraft or to the U-boats. There was an agreed limit of, I believe, ten or fifteen miles for trawlers fishing legitimately, but this chap was way outside those limits.

It was a very difficult decision for the leader of our formation to make. We had been told that anything of this sort was fair game but the trawler did look very defenceless. However, orders is orders, and the leader ordered an attack. We each gave it a burst as we flew over it and then pressed on, leaving it still afloat but smoking.

We had been flying for four hours and fifteen minutes by the time we landed. The low flying over the sea had been very tiring for the pilots and all of us felt that our eyeballs were popping out with the constant strain of searching sea and sky. After this trip we found that special tinted glasses which were provided for us were a great help.

The next day was spent swimming and sunbathing. The day after, however, we were off at eight o'clock in the morning. Ben and I were to lead a formation of four Mozzies on a patrol which would take us within sight of the north-west coast of Spain. As Flight Commander, Ben would naturally be called upon to lead some of these patrols. It meant, however, that with my exceedingly small mount of navigational experience I would have to accept the main responsibility for the navigation. Still, I had long ago realised that common sense was perhaps the most valuable asset for a navigator, and so we would have to hope for the best. Luckily, Coastal Command received very good, reliable forecasts of wind and weather which helped immensely.

On this patrol we were not detailed to look for any particular target. In order to cover as large an area of sea and sky as possible, we flew in very loose formation. Ben, as leader, had his Number Two about half a mile away, behind and to starboard.

Number Three was level with us and a mile or so to starboard, while Number Four was half a mile behind and to starboard of Number Three. If something came into sight over to starboard our Number Three would become leader and we would act as his Number Three.

As we were within sight of the Spanish coast, I was able to check my navigation visually and found that we were pretty well on track. We turned to fly parallel to the coast, some twenty miles from it, but by the time we had finished this leg of our flight we had seen nothing. We turned for the long sea leg home and had been flying for some ten minutes when Number Three spotted an aircraft on his starboard side. It was just a speck at first, but as we opened our throttles for the chase it got rapidly bigger. We were soon able to identify it as a Focke Wulf Kondor, the military version of the Kurier.

It was an enormous four-engined aircraft, heading out into the Atlantic, and it made no attempt to get away until it was much too late. It was a beautiful day again with just a few white clouds at about three thousand feet over towards the land.

The Mosquitos came screaming in at full speed. The Kondor's crew was keeping a poor look-out or else their aircraft recognition needed brushing up. They kept coming towards us. Probably the last thing they were expecting to meet so far down in the Bay of Biscay was us. The leading Mozzie was almost within firing range before the Kondor realised that something was amiss. It went into a very tight turn in an effort to make for safer parts – much too late, for the leading Mozzie was already pumping shells into him. Seconds later the next Mozzie was assisting.

In no time at all large chunks of Kondor were falling off. Before Ben could get near enough for a shot, down into the sea went the enemy aircraft streaming black smoke behind it. We watched it crash and part of it floated for some seconds, with a great pall of black smoke hanging over it.

Two days later we set off on what promised to be a real thriller. We were leader of the second section of four Mozzies in a formation of eight. A pack of five U-boats had been reported way down in the Bay. A strike force of Coastal Command bombers was going after them. It was thought probable that the U-boats would have a cover of Junkers 88s and we were to deal with them. As so often happens when hopes are built up, it all fizzled out. Neither the Mozzies nor the strike force saw anything at all.

Fighter Command decided that instead of maintaining the composite squadron at Pedannack, it would be better to loan a night-fighter squadron. The squadron selected was 141 Squadron and we had just one more patrol before being recalled to 157 Squadron. This time, however, the weather was poor and we made an early return.

When we returned to our squadron there had been some changes. They had moved from Bradwell Bay to Hunsdon, in Hertfordshire, and at last Fighter Command had realised the futility of continuing with Mark 5 A.I. They were to scrap it and we were to get Mark 4 in its place. This was very welcome news.

We flew on an Intruder patrol of St Trond airfield, near the German border in Belgium, on June 26th. Wuppertal, to the east of the Ruhr, was being bombed, and although we saw lots of activity in that direction, St Trond was silent as the grave.

July turned out to be quite an eventful month. The first of the Mark 4 equipped Mozzies arrived, to everyone's joy. On July 2nd we were on defensive patrol with Mark 4s. Although no Huns appeared we had two grand runs with G.C.I. and felt full of the joys of spring.

Next night we were off on an Intruder patrol of St Trond again. It was a low-level patrol and my navigation was spot on. We arrived at our patrol point, a few miles west of the airfield, dead on time and dead on track. We were happy to see several lights on the airfield and began our figure-of-eight patrol. Nobody seemed to be taking any notice of us, so we edged over a little closer. After a few minutes Ben said urgently:

'Hey, what's that? There's something moving down there.'

'Can't see anything . . . Oh yes, I can. The other side of the airfield. Is that it?'

'That's it all right. That's a pair of navigation lights, chum. I'll bet he's taxying round to take off. Let's have a dekko at the target map.'

I spread out the special map of St Trond airfield that we had collected from Intelligence. Ben studied it.

'There's the runway they'll be using. See, he's nearly at the end of it now. Here, take this.'

He whipped the Mozzie round into position with perfect judgement. Down we dived just as the aircraft on the ground turned on to the runway. We could see it gathering speed as its engines were opened up. The clot still had his navigation lights on; perhaps we would be able to put them out for him.

They must have realised on the ground what was about to happen. A series of two-star red Very lights were fired in quick succession from the ground. By this time our dive had brought us just behind and below the other aircraft. It was a Dornier 217 about three hundred feet up.

As Ben opened fire a two-star white Very light came from the Dornier. A long burst of cannons brought strikes all along the fuselage as the Dornier went straight down. It crashed with a large explosion half a mile from the end of the runway.

Three searchlights flickered up from the airfield, searching for us. But we were no longer there. After a few minutes we were back on our figure-of-eight patrol and the searchlights went out. So did all the other lights on the airfield. We were able to maintain our position quite well, however, by the fire of the Dornier, which burned for the further half-hour we were on patrol. Occasionally the proceedings were livened up as ammunition or bombs exploded.

I was sent to Ford, in Sussex, for the ten-day Navigator Leader course on July 13th. I must have done reasonably well, for soon after my return I was told that I would be posted as Navigator Leader to 488 New Zealand Squadron and would fly with their C.O. 488 Squadron were at Drem, in Scotland; I was to report there on August 8th.

At first I was very brassed off about this posting. I would become a Flight Lieutenant, but I was due for that, anyway, at the end of August. Also Ben and I were getting on so well now that it seemed silly to waste our experience. However, I had learned the wisdom of bowing to the inevitable, so that although I could not pretend to like the idea of the posting I gave up worrying about it.

Ben and I did a couple of defensive patrols which were uneventful and an Intruder patrol. This was notable only because it was the first time we had flown over Germany itself.

At the end of July Ben went off on leave. I hoped like the devil that we would somehow be able to get together on a squadron again. For the time being, though, it was goodbye.

I did flying tests with two others pilots in preparation for Intruder patrols, but the weather was bad and both trips were called off. I was particularly sorry that the second one had to be cancelled. Not only was it arranged for my last day with 157 Squadron, but I was to have flown with the Squadron Commander. He was quite a character and I would dearly have loved to have carried out an operational sortie with him.

I have mentioned earlier that Pop Wheeler had been awarded the M.C. and Bar in the First War and the D.F.C. in this. Recently he had won the Bar to his D.F.C. He had a great hatred for the Germans. I believe that he lost a brother in the First War; certainly, when he flew over enemy territory, he never brought back any ammunition with him.

On one trip he had been over Germany he found on his way back that he still had a few rounds left. He remembered having heard that the Casino at Knocke had been taken over for the use of U-boat crews. He therefore asked his navigator to give him a course to steer for Knocke, although it was miles off their route. It appeared that the Wingco knew Knocke very well, so he proceeded to the Casino and used up the ammunition.

Whilst there was a war on he was interested only in operational flying and he just could not get enough of that. On every possible occasion he leapt into the air and always took the patrols that would take him over Germany. He was flying so often at one stage that Fighter Command had to restrain him with a series of very strongly worded signals.

Not long after I left 157 Squadron he was posted to a non-operational job, where he sulked for a short time. He then managed to pull some strings and wangled himself into an operational flying job in Bomber Command. He was posted 'missing' after a big raid on Cologne. We all found it difficult to believe somehow that such a character could be dead. He had become an almost legendary figure and I always imagined that he would turn up having organised his own private army behind the German lines.

I made my farewells to 157 Squadron and set off for Drem, where I found the most awful shambles. I met the C.O. with whom I was to fly, Wing Commander Burton-Gyles, D.S.O., D.F.C., an extremely pleasant and capable young man. He was, unfortunately, killed later flying from Malta.

He informed me that he would brief me a little later about my job, but at the moment he had a rather difficult interview on his hands. A clot of a sergeant pilot had, the day before, landed a Beaufighter. While he was still running along the runway, he had, for some unknown reason, pulled up his under-carriage, thereby doing no good at all to the said Beaufighter. The Wingco had torn the sergeant off a frightful strip and had ordered him to report to his office next day to receive another. The next morning, on the very day I arrived, the Wingco had been airborne in a Beau and had committed the selfsame offence as the sergeant pilot. I had put in my appearance just a few seconds before the interview was to take place.

Whatever was said, the interview was soon over and the Wingco put me in the picture. He had been until recently a Flight Commander on an Intruder squadron and had no experience of A.I. He had been called for an interview at Fighter Command, where he had been told that he was to be posted in as C.O. of the New Zealand night-fighter squadron, Number 488. Morale was rather low on the squadron and he was to sort it out. They would give all the help they could, and

Mr Jordan, the New Zealand High Commissioner, could probably be very useful.

He had joined 488 Squadron in June 1943, and found the reason for the low morale pretty obvious. The squadron was fed-up with doing almost nothing. They had been formed in June 1942 at Church Fenton in Yorkshire, and in September of that year had moved to Heathfield, where I had originally joined 141 Squadron. There they had remained, getting more and more fed-up with the lack of action. They were supposed to be a defensive night-fighter squadron, but had not had a single chase on an enemy aircraft since they had been formed. There was just nothing doing at Heathfield.

The only operational flying any of them carried out had been on Ranger patrols and they felt completely out of the real war. They had achieved a fair amount of success against trains and lorries on the Ranger patrols, but the New Zealanders, anyhow, had come an awful long way to fight in this war, and they wanted really to come to grips with the enemy.

Wing Commander Burton-Gyles summed up the situation right away and got in touch with Mr Jordan. A meeting was arranged in London and the Wingco had been given an opening straight away. The High Commissioner had asked him how the boys were and if there was anything they wanted. The Wingco told him in no uncertain terms that the boys were fed-up with flying obsolescent Beaufighters on a non-operational station and that they wanted to fly Mosquitos on a station that was operational.

Mr Jordon thought for a moment, and then said that in a day or two he would be dining with Mr Winston Churchill. He would see what he could do.

He was able to do quite a lot, for in July 488 Squadron found themselves right at the top of the priority list for re-equipping with the latest Mozzies.

They had moved to Drem early in August, and when I arrived the re-equipping had just begun. The Wingco had asked for an experienced navigator as leader, who would also fly with him in order that he himself should become operational with the new equipment as soon as possible. The new Mozzies were fitted with Mark 8 A.I., a slightly modified version of Mark 7. I was the only navigator with experience of this type of A.I., and even the Special Signals section, who dealt with the servicing of A.I., had no knowledge of its workings.

The Special Signals Officer was sent off on a hurried course with a few picked men, and a 'circus', a travelling Mark 8 school, visited us at Drem for a week or two. I had to set in motion an intensive training programme and also to fly with the Wingco at every available opportunity. By dint of much hard effort all round things had started to fall into slightly better shape towards the end of the month.

On August 26th three bombshells fell upon us in quick succession. Wing Commander Burton-Gyles was posted to command 23 Squadron at Malta. Our Special Signals Officer, having just completed his Mark 8 course, was repatriated to New Zealand, and we were told that on September 3rd we would be moved to Bradwell Bay, right in the front line.

Move we did – without a C.O. or a Special Signals Officer and still not fully re-equipped with Mozzies. However, we were now in 11 Group of Fighter Command. They rallied round with lectures and briefings, for there was a great deal for these very keen chaps to learn. A new C.O. and Special Signals Officer were posted in and more new crews arrived to bring the squadron up to full strength. Some of these new crews were not trained on Mozzies or on Mark 8 A.I., so that training had to go on apace.

Although 488 was a New Zealand Squadron, most of the navigators were British, as were almost all the ground crews. When I joined them, the only British pilots were, I believe, the C.O. and one of the Flight Commanders. The new C.O. was Wing Commander Peter Hamley, A.F.C., who was also British. He was a very experienced day pilot who had been C.O. of a Spitfire O.T.U. He had completed a short course at Cranfield, one of the night-fighter O.T.U.s, and it had been intended that he should spend three months as a super-numerary on an operational night-fighter squadron, before being posted to one

118

as C.O. The crisis on 488 Squadron had meant that he had to be posted in to us straight from Cranfield where he had crewed up with a pupil navigator.

Just as the previous C.O. had done, he asked me to fly with him so that he might become operational as soon as possible. He was a very easy chap to get on with, and I explained that if possible I would very much like to recrew with Ben at some later stage. He agreed to see what could be done about this when the time arose.

Fortunately we had almost a fortnight without enemy activity and we were able to carry on with intensive training. The chaps were tremendously keen and I felt sure that there was plenty of ability too; nothing could replace experience, however, so practice, practice and more practice was the catchword.

The Wingco had decided not to put himself on the night operational programme until he had quite a bit of practice with me. In the meantime, I did three defensive patrols with Flight Lieutenant Ball, a very experienced night pilot whose navigator was on sick leave. We had some useful practice, but there were no Huns around.

On the night of September 15th I was having dinner in the mess with the Wingco when he said that he thought it would be a good idea if we spent an hour or two at dispersal with the Duty Flight. I could introduce him to any one he did not know, and it was undoubtedly the best way for him to get acquainted with the aircrews.

After dinner we set off in the Wingco's staff car for 'B' Flight dispersal. There seemed to be lots of activity on the airfield, but we were quite unprepared for the scene that met our eyes when we arrived at 'B' Flight. There was a terrific hullabaloo. Ground and aircrews were yelling and dancing around with joy. Almost exactly a year after the squadron's formation the very first enemy aircraft had been shot down.

The excitement and enthusiasm were understandable. After a minute or two we managed to get the story. Two Mozzies had been up on patrol, practising with G.C.I., when some Bandits had appeared. Flight Lieutenant Jimmy Gunn, one of the most popular pilots on the squadron, had been the successful pilot. Four more Mozzies had been scrambled but all the activity was now over.

The combat had taken place just north of Bradwell. Just as when Ben and I had a similar combat in much the same place, it had been watched by the excited chaps at dispersal. They had heard the cannon fire, followed by the sight of an aircraft going down in flames. An R/T set which had been fitted up in dispersal had enabled them to listen to the Controller actually putting Jimmy on to a bomber. They had heard his triumphant 'Tally ho!' when he sighted it. This had been the cause for the jubilation in which we joined.

Hardly anyone noticed when the C.O. was called into the Flight Office to speak on the telephone. I did, though, and I also noticed that he was trying to catch my eye as he stood in the doorway, with a serious expression on his face. He motioned me to go into the office with him.

'That was Control on the phone just then,' he said. 'They're a bit worried about Gunn. They haven't been able to raise him on R/T since the combat and they are afraid that he might have bought it. What do you think the form is? I certainly hate to tell the chaps unless we are sure.'

Remembering my own experience when the R/T had packed up, I suggested that we might wait a little longer. We asked Control to let us have any news immediately. We checked with Bradwell Flying Control. They had not heard from Gunn. Then the ops telephone rang. Two aircraft had been reported going down together, both in flames. The C.O. had no option but to tell the sad news, which was only partly lightened by the fact that Jimmy had certainly got his Hun.

Most of the crews who had been airborne had now landed. They were in the crew room, discarding flying kit and joining in the still excited buzz of conversation. I called for quiet, which was not all that easy to obtain . The C.O. made his announcement. A shocked air of gloom followed a brief moment of disbelief.

Into the quietened crew room came Flight Lieutenant Ron Watts and his navigator. They had been in the Mozzie on patrol with Jimmy Gunn when the raiders had appeared and had heard what had happened on their own R/T. When Jimmy had not responded to Control, they realised what had occurred.

I wandered over to them as they replaced their kit in their flying lockers. Watts and his navigator, Flying Officer Folley, were both quiet, unassuming types.

'What sort of trip did you have?' I asked. 'Did you get a chase?'

'Well, er, yes. We got a Dornier 217!'

The atmosphere brightened considerably. In a moment questions were being hurled at the successful pair. I felt sure that Jimmy Gunn would have been glad that his comrades were thus given a chance to snap out of their gloom. It was confirmed later that a Heinkel 111 and a Mozzie had crashed together. We had the satisfaction of knowing that Jimmy had made his kill.

Things were pretty quiet for the next month and we persevered with training. I got quite a few hours in with the C.O.; my flying hours had jumped to over five hundred day and two hundred night. On October 23rd the Wingco and I were ordered off with another crew on an absolute stinker of a night. Something was alleged to have been plotted so off we went. It was pouring with rain and the clouds were very low indeed. We were in cloud almost as soon as our wheels left the runway. Up we went to eighteen thousand feet, still in cloud with lightning flashing all around us and the Mozzie being thrown all over the place.

Suddenly the whole aircraft was bathed in the weirdest blue light. Little balls of blue fire were dancing over our windscreen, along our wings and making our propellers look for all the world like giant Catherine wheels. I had heard of St Elmo's Fire; so this was what it looked like. It was most eerie. If I had been in the mood for reading I could have read the smallest print quite easily, so vivid was the light.

It stayed with us for quite a time; then after we had been

patrolling for about half an hour, during which time we had never been out of cloud, we were ordered to return to base – an order which we thankfully obeyed.

Soon after I became Navigator Leader I had noticed that there was a navigator on the operational strength of the squadron by the name of Flight Lieutenant Clarke, whom I had not yet met. On enquiry I was informed that he was in hospital, having sustained a cracked skull earlier in the year.

When he eventually returned he reported to my office and I found him a very pleasant and amusing little chap. Evidently his skull had mended reasonably quickly. The main reason for his long absence had been not so much the cracked skull but the fact that the Royal Air Force medicos were highly suspicious of aircrew who had experienced hard bumps on their noggins. They subjected them to many interviews with psychiatrists about whom Clarke had several good stories.

The one that amused me most, however, did not concern the headshrinkers. He had been in a ward of an R.A.F. hospital when the Princess Royal visited it. The ward was full of injured aircrew.

'The trouble was,' he said, 'she asked each chap how he was getting on and how he had received his injury.'

'What was wrong with that?' I asked.

'Well,' came the answer, 'most of the other chaps had been wounded in combat, or jumped out of blazing aircraft or something equally heroic. I fractured my skull, falling backwards off a bar stool at a New Year's Eve party in the mess.'

I never did find out what he told the Princess Royal.

Chapter IX

RADIO COUNTER-MEASURES

THE squadron bagged two more Huns in November although nothing ever happened when we were up. Ben flew in to see me with the news that 157 Squadron was to move to Predannack at the end of November. They were rather brassed off at the prospect. He had lunch with us and we discussed with the Wingco the chances of a posting for Ben to our squadron. The Wingco pointed out the policy of having New Zealand pilots as far as possible.

Ben and I found that we would both be on leave in London at the end of the month so we arranged to meet. He had never been over a film studio so I laid on a visit to Denham studios. Two films were being made there; Noel Coward was working on that grand film, *In Which We Serve*, and his play *Blithe Spirit* was also being filmed.

On one of the large stages we saw an almost life-size replica of the destroyer *Kelly*, which was most impressive. It had been built on tubular scaffolding which was so arranged that the ship could rock from side to side to an angle of forty-five degrees. We were allowed a good look round and found it extremely interesting. The destroyer's guns were made almost entirely of wood, yet all the moving parts worked and it was possible to insert a dummy shell. The gun would then show all the motions of a real gun being fired.

From there we went on to the set where a scene from *Blithe Spirit* was being shot. We watched Kay Hammond, in ghostly

123

make-up, playing a couple of scenes. The ghost make-up reminded me of Bob Donat and *The Ghost Goes West.*

One of the features on a New Zealand squadron such as Bradwell was the food. We had the normal R.A.F. food, which was pretty good on the whole, but, in addition to this, we all shared in the simply wonderful parcels these lads were sent from home. When we were having our night-flying supper at dispersal there would be on the table as extras a colossal spread of rich fruit cakes, honey, butter, jams, tinned food – especially tinned oysters which were great favourites with the New Zealanders – and almost everything else that it was possible to pack and send.

In addition to all this, most airfields, and Bradwell in particular, seemed to be first-class mushroom fields. Most evenings in late summer and through the autumn we would fill our caps with mushrooms on our way to dispersal. The only injury I received throughout the war was to my digestion. It was well worth it, though.

The Wingco and I flew many hours on many patrols, but we were not destined to have much excitement. We had only one chase after a Hun, and that was after a long pursuit one night in early December, when we had a visual on a Messerschmitt 410. The wretched thing spotted us before the Wingco could get lined up for a shot and it dived away much too fast for us.

At the end of December the Wingco was told he would be posted to a job that meant promotion for him. So keen had he become on night fighting, however, that he tried hard but unsuccessfully to have the posting put off. Before he left he kept his promise and arranged with 11 Group that I should be given the choice of rejoining Ben or crewing up with the new C.O. who had just arrived to take over command of 488 Squadron.

Although I was not terribly thrilled with the idea of going to Predannack, I knew that 157 Squadron would not be there forever. I had flown with many pilots on 488 Squadron, some good, some bad, but I had always felt somehow that my destiny was bound up with Ben. In the meantime I had to remain as Navigator Leader while the situation was sorted out at 11 Group Headquarters.

I received the following very pleasant letter from Peter Hamley, now a Group Captain:

8th January 1944.
Dear Brandy,

As I had to nip smartly into a taxi before some Yanks got it, I did not have a chance to say goodbye, so I am writing to thank you for all the help you gave me whilst at Bradwell in becoming operational quickly, and also all the loyal support you gave me as my Navigator Leader.

I spoke at 11 Group about Benson. It appears that 29 Squadron has its full complement of squadron leaders and 11 Group are not agitating to get him back. So you will have to make up your mind whether you want to fly with Wing Commander Haine or go down to Predannack with him. As I told you, now would appear to be the time to decide, as I know Haine would be happy to fly with you.

Well, Brandy, I hope to come down to Bradwell soon to see all the chaps. Thanking you again for your cheerful help and enthusiasm.

Yours Ever.

Sure enough, next morning I had a phone call from 11 Group, asking me what I wished to do. They would have to arrange the posting and a replacement for me. They had checked with 157 Squadron, who would be glad to have me back, but I would not be posted in as Navigator Leader, as they already had one. When I said that I would like to rejoin Ben at Predannack, they told me that I might have to wait about a month so that I could hand over to my replacement when they found one.

Things worked out according to schedule. I flew with the new C.O. three or four times and did a couple of patrols with one of the pilots whose navigator had 'flu. Then on January 23rd, 1944, this pilot flew me to Predannack.

488 (New Zealand) Squadron were to make quite a name for themselves later, for they became part of the Allied Expeditionary Air Force and operated with great success. In spite of

the fact that they had no opportunity to fly against the enemy until their move to Bradwell in September 1943, by the time the squadron was disbanded in April 1945 they had destroyed no fewer than sixty-seven enemy aircraft, with three probables and eleven damaged.

During this time they lost only four crews in action and eleven in flying accidents – a very creditable record indeed and I am proud to have served with them as Navigator Leader, even if only for a comparatively short time. They were a grand bunch of fellows.

The squadron mess at Predannack was the Pollurian Hotel, which was about five miles from the airfield and only some ten minutes' walk from beautiful Mullion Cove.

The squadron had done very well in the two months they had been there. They had been engaged in Instep patrols, as the long-range day patrols in the Bay of Biscay were now known. They had destroyed seven enemy aircraft, with one probable and four damaged. There was obviously a fair bit of action to be had, but in spite of that most of the fellows wanted to get back on to their primary job of night fighting for which they had trained so hard.

Although Ben had done a considerable amount of flying in the five months we had been separated, he had not enjoyed any success at all. This added substance to my firm convictions about splitting up successful crews.

He had quite a lot to tell me. The squadron whom 157 Squadron had relieved was 141 Squadron, on which we had done our first tour. They were commanded by Wing Commander Bob Braham, who finished the war as the second highest scoring night-fighter pilot, with no less than three D.S.O.s and three D.F.C.s.

There was a story about him that deserves to be true. He walked into the bar of an officers' mess one day, wearing battle-dress on which he was wearing only the ribbons of these two decorations, the two bars to each being denoted by little silver rosettes on the ribbons.

An American officer in the bar, observing this phenomenon, was heard to remark:

'Say, who is that guy? He's only wearing a couple of gongs, but they sure are riveted on.'

Ben told me another story about Braham which I later verified. From 1942 onwards the Middle East night-fighter squadrons were being built up and the Home squadrons were asked fairly regularly for crews to volunteer for such postings. When Bob Braham took over as C.O. of 141 Squadron, one of the sergeant navigators rejoiced in the name of Perfect.

Sergeant Perfect did not particularly wish to go to the Middle East, but as a result of several misunderstandings he found himself scheduled to go there as navigator to a pilot who was extremely keen to go.

Sergeant Perfect whipped in an application to see the C.O. This was Bob Braham, of course, and it happened that he had already asked to see Perfect and his pilot to wish them good luck.

Sergent Perfect found himself in front of the C.O. and the following conversation ensued:

'Ah! Sergeant *Prefect*, so you are keen to go to the Middle East.'

'*Perfect*,' corrected the sergeant.

'Jolly good show! I wish you the best of luck,' rejoined the C.O.

Sergeant Perfect found himself outside the door bound for the Middle East and wondering how it all happened.

Ben and one of the Flight Commanders had discussed the possibility of an Intruder sortie to an airfield near Bordeaux. There was a large lake nearby and Intelligence thought that long-range German convoy spotters were based on the airfield with some flying-boats on the lake, called Lake Biscarosse. They had asked for permission to try an Intruder patrol, but for various reasons permission had been refused. They had been told, however, than an application might be made later. When Ben knew for certain that I was on my way down he put in a fresh request and had been given permission to try the patrol at the first suitable opportunity.

We flew on an Instep patrol as leader of four Mozzies on January 30th. We spent nearly four hours patrolling some fifty miles to the south-west of Ireland, where some Junkers 88s were thought to carry out an occasional patrol. We saw nothing at all.

On February 5th the weather looked just right for our Bordeaux trip and at 19.30 hours we set off on the near-six-hundred-mile sea journey to Bordeaux. We flew at two hundred feet, well to the west of the Brest Peninsula as we did not want to be plotted by the enemy raid-warning system; we meant our presence in the Bay to come as a complete surprise to the Hun. The flight to our target would take us two hours twenty minutes, leaving us about twenty minutes' patrol time and plenty of flying time in hand for our return journey.

Everything worked out very well from the navigational angle. We kept some forty miles out to sea all down the west coast of France, and when we finally turned east for our target we saw that we were crossing the coast as planned, about eight miles south of Lake Biscarosse. There was a moon, but rather too much cloud in the whole area for our liking. We climbed to two thousand feet over the coast and the lake showed up very well. Just to the north-east was the airfield of Bordeaux/ Merignac, and close by was the town of Bordeaux itself, absolutely ablaze with lights. They were obviously not worried about black-out regulations there – it was the very first time I had seen a town lighted up since I had begun flying.

There were several lights on the airfield but we saw nothing moving. After a ten-minute patrol there, we had a look at the lake. Unfortunately, cloud was tending to obscure the moon and we could see nothing on the lake. We did three or four runs over it before deciding that it was useless; then we had another look at the airfield. Again we could see nothing moving and so we dived low across it to see if we could spot any parked aircraft. It was too dark. We could not see a thing.

Nobody took any notice of us – we were probably thought to be a Junkers 88 wanting to land. It seemed a pity to have brought all our ammunition all this way just to take it home again, but that was what we very regretfully did. The homeward trip was quite uneventful. We were disappointed, but felt that it had been a worthwhile effort and determined to try again if we could.

One of the Flight Commanders, Squadron Leader Tappin, and his Navigator, Flying Officer Thomas, did the same trip two nights later. As they turned in to the French coast just south of Lake Biscarosse they saw a large aircraft with navigation lights on. It was flying near the lake. As they darted in they recognised to their delight and amazement that it was a six-engined Blohm and Voss 222 flying-boat.

It was so enormous that Tappin's first burst of fire fell short simply because he could not believe that he was so far from it. He soon rectified his mistake, popped in closer and picked off the engines on one side, one by one – very satisfying.

Just after this I went off on leave to be married but that is no part of this story. Suffice to say that we took advantage of a very generous scheme initiated by Lord Nuffield, whereby aircrew and their families could stay for a holiday at any one of several of the best hotels in Britain for a nominal charge. We stayed at the Lygon Arms in the beautiful Cotswold village of Broadway.

I returned to Predannack at the end of February and we carried out half a dozen more Instep patrols, all of them fairly uneventful. On one of these we chased after three spots on the horizon, one after another, only to find a Liberator and two Sunderlands.

In the middle of March the squadron received the glad tidings that we were to move to Valley, in Anglesey. We were to re-equip with the newest Mozzies carrying the latest A.I. for a new and very special job. The A.I. was Mark 10 and we would be told details of the job at a later stage.

Mark 10 A.I. was an American production. Early in the war the basic principles of A.I. had been presented to them; we had carried on development on lines which had brought forth Mark 8 A.I., whilst the Americans had developed Mark 10, which they referred to as *SCR* 720. We were to find that it had many advantages and only a few disadvantages compared to the British Mark 8.

On March 28th a Mark 10 'circus' arrived to enable the navigators to learn something about it. This circus was under the command of Squadron Leader Hoy, D.F.C., and was run very efficiently. It consisted of six Wellingtons fitted up as flying classrooms and enabled us to get down to some pretty intensive training. Mark 10 had a greater range and better coverage than anything I had previously used, but it had two tubes to watch and lots and lots of knobs to twiddle. It worked all right, but it would certainly need a great deal of practice and the ideal operator for it would be one with three arms and three eyes. No extra arms or eyes were included in the squadron's re-equipment, so we would just have to get down to some hard practice.

I managed to get rather more than my share of flying in the Wellingtons by getting myself taken on as an extra instructor after my first couple of trips. I was really delighted with Mark 10 A.I.; the more I tried it, the more I realised that it was exactly what we needed from the start: long-range, good coverage, reliability, an excellent beacon facility for homings, and it was difficult enough to use properly to make it a constant challenge. I could hardly wait to try it in a Mozzie, but we were not due to get them until early May.

So we did not wait. Ben had been wondering what it was all about and I kept him informed of what I thought of it. Somehow he obtained permission for us to try to fly to Ford, where 456 (Australian) Squadron had just begun to re-equip with Mozzies with Mark 10. We met several friends and acquaintances in the mess and spent a rather liquid night in the bar during which time we managed to persuade the C.O. of 456 Squadron to let us have a flip in one of his precious new Mozzies on the morrow.

We duly had our flight the next afternoon in a Mozzie with the new magic box; I hope Ben was suitably impressed. From my log book I see that we did not return straight home from

Ford but flew to Coltishall, another night-fighter station. We spent the night there – I am not sure why, but perhaps it was in the hope that we might wangle another trip in a Mark 10-equipped Mozzie, or to see if the squadron there was experiencing any snags with Mark 10.

We returned in the fullness of time to Valley, where we learned that on May 4th the Squadron would be moving to Swanington, near Norwich. We would be transferred to Bomber Command from Fighter Command and would be in 100 Group, known as the Radio Countermeasures Group. The new job on which we would be engaged was Bomber Support operations. We were certainly getting plenty of variety in this war.

The move to Swanington duly took place and we began to learn something of our new role. Wing Commander 'Sammy' Hoare had been attached to the squadron for a few weeks to initiate yet another bout of intensive training. He wore the ribbons of the D.S.O. and D.F.C. and was quite a character. Although he had only one eye, he managed to see better, even in the dark, than most people with two. He had experienced great success as an Intruder pilot and had commanded an Intruder squadron.

He sported a truly magnificent ginger moustache. When confronted by a moustache almost as good, he was once heard to mutter:

'Huh! Fluff, my boy. Fluff. Why, it's not a moustache at all unless both wingtips can be seen from behind.'

Our first new Mozzie arrived on May 7th. Sammy Hoare grabbed it and asked me to demonstrate this A.I. stuff to him. He had to make a couple of calls in the South of England; so on the way south, we did a few practice interceptions on any aircraft that came our way.

Our final call was at Tangmere, right on the South Coast. All around there, for as far as I could see, every field was packed tight with lorries, tanks, barges and all sorts of weird-looking objects. There was so much equipment down there that it seemed that this little island must tip up with all this weight at one end. What a target all this would have been for Hitler's flying bomb.

Once our first new Mozzie had arrived the others started coming in quickly and we proceeded to make the best possible use of them. Not only did we all have to brush up our navigation and master Mark 10 A.I., but these new Mozzies were fitted with a navigational aid called 'Gee', which was new to us. It was fairly easy to operate and it enabled the user to obtain a fix of his position very quickly. Its coverage extended pretty well all over the British Isles and deep into enemy territory. Altogether it was a very useful piece of equipment to carry on the job for which we were training.

157 Squadron was joined at Swanington by 85 Squadron, one of the crack defensive night-fighter squadrons, and a spirit of fairly friendly rivalry sprang up between the two squadrons. We had more experience of operating over enemy territory, but 85 Squadron were in far better A.I. practice than we were.

We had been told that most of our patrols for our new job would be at high level, probably at about eighteen thousand feet. The patrols would be carried out in bad as well as good weather and the timing and navigation would have to be spot on. This was all new for us, so Ben and I went off on another series of cross-country exercises, but this time they were at high level. They went off quite well, and what with these trips, Mark 10 and Gee practices, our time was pretty well taken up.

By this time we had been briefed about our new role and it would perhaps be as well to explain what it was all about and how it had come to pass. In order to do this it is necessary to anticipate the shape of things to come, as well as to look back a bit.

One of the most fascinating stories of the war is that of the constant battle that went on between British and German scientists in the field of radar and signals. In this battle there would appear to be ample evidence that our boffins were always quite a good way ahead of the enemy. There was a positive and a negative side to the battle. The positive side was the provision of control, communication and warning systems and navigational aids to one's own aircraft. The negative side was to attempt to ensure that the similar aids possessed by the enemy were hindered or jammed in some way, so that they were as little use as possible to them.

On the positive side for us were the Long Range Warning System, V.H.F. radio, G.C.I. control, and finally A.I. – all of which had helped to make it possible for Fighter Command to carry out its job. Other equally valuable inventions had been produced for Bomber and Coastal Commands, but they are beyond the scope of this book. The negative side of the work of our boffins must now be considered.

The big German night bomber raids of 1940 and early 1941 had shown up the weakness of our night defences, but it had also indicated that the German navigators needed navigational aids for any but the easiest targets. Raids on the big coastal towns of the East and South Coasts, or on London with the Thames Estuary as a guide, were one thing. Finding an inland town, such as Derby or Birmingham, was quite another matter.

To assist their bomber crews, the German boffins had produced a device known as *Knickebein*. This navigational aid was based on the use of two shortwave radio beams directed on the target for the night. They would be operated from points well apart, say one from Holland and the other from France, so that the intersection of the beams was exactly over the target. The technique used was for the bomber to set course roughly for the target. He would listen for either of the two beams, which he would hear in his earphones as 'dots' or 'dashes'. Whichever he heard first he would know from his briefing which beam it was and he could then fly along it listening to the sound until the other beam started to come in. When the two sounds in his earphones became a steady combined note, he could release his bombs, for he had reached the point of intersection of the beams. Fairly accurate blind-bombing through cloud was possible with this device.

The first round in the radio countermeasures battle went to our boffins when they discovered the existence of this beam system before it was actually used operationally by the German bombers at night. They experimented with the possibility of jamming it without much success. This was as well perhaps, for the enemy would have known then that the beam was being mucked about. They then decided that the best thing to do was to bend the beam so that the intersection was somewhere quite different to the place the Germans had intended to attack.

This was effected by picking up one of the beams and re-broadcasting it in a slightly different direction. This scheme worked very well on several occasions and had the advantage that there was no reason for the enemy to suspect that the beams were being tampered with. One of the outstanding successes was when aircraft attempting a raid on Liverpool were induced to drop their bombs in the Irish Sea.

As the raids on this country became fewer and the main accent shifted on to Bomber Command's offensive role, the task for our boffins became that of helping to make things as easy as possible for the crews of Bomber Command. The Germans had a fairly similar set-up for Long Range Warning and Ground Control to our own. Our boffins set to work to find out the various frequencies which were being used by the enemy and then to produce apparatus which would jam them sufficiently to make them useless.

Obtaining this information was a long and difficult job. Ground stations listened out for enemy transmissions day and night. At the same time almost every Bomber Command raid had one or more aircraft fitted up with listening apparatus and notes were made of transmissions over a very wide band. These notes were sorted out and our boffins would then decide what new types of equipment were being installed by the enemy and for what purpose they were being used. As soon as this was done, a jamming device would be evolved and very soon with every Bomber Command raid there would be a few aircraft carrying loads of the various jamming devices designed to jam every bit of radar and signals equipment used by the Germans.

The main threat to our bombers was the enemy night fighter. The whole idea of our boffins was to make everything just as difficult for them as it was humanly possible, for nearly all of

Bomber Command's effort was to take place at night. Their main raids were carried out on the theory of 'saturation' bombing. That is to say, a large number of bombers would drop their bombs on a target in as short a space of time as possible.

The tactics of the German night bombers when they were operating over Britain had been based mainly on the idea of sending waves of bombers over in relatively small numbers in order to keep the Alert going in our big cities for as long as possible. Once our night defence became reasonably competent it was not called upon to deal with mass raids such as the Luftwaffe now found themselves faced with.

In their attempts to deal with the very heavy raids they experienced as the war developed, the Luftwaffe evolved two main methods of interception: route interception and target interception. Route interception was an attempt to assemble as many twin-engined fighters as possible as soon as a raid was detected and to bring them into our bomber stream, either on the inward or outward route.

This was done with the aid of instructions from the ground and a running commentary on the progress of the raid broadcast over the R/T. The instructions gave the fighters courses to steer and were usually given by reference to radio or visual beacons which had been suitably placed to cover the whole of Germany. Once the fighters were in our bomber stream they had their A.I. with which they could carry out interception on their own. The more skilful crews were used as leaders and equipped with the best apparatus available. They endeavoured to get into the bomber stream at the earliest possible moment and dropped 'fighter flares' to guide the lesser brethren.

Target interception consisted of putting as many fighters as possible over the anticipated target. This method would be used in bright moonlight conditions when single-engined single-seater fighters could be used, or when insufficient early warning had been obtained to feed fighters into the bomber stream on the inward route. They would operate with the aid of flares from the leader fighters, visual signals from the ground such as searchlights pointing towards the expected target and

135

the running commentary which consisted of a summing up of all the available information.

In order to 'frustrate their knavish tricks' our boffins had to study each stage of the operation. The Long Range Warning System that the Germans had thrown all round Fortress Europe was comparatively easy to jam, either from ground stations in England or by patrols of jamming aircraft flying over the Channel and the North Sea.

Communications, ground-to-air and air-to-ground radio, were jammed in much the same way and, in addition, aircraft filled with jamming apparatus would fly with the bombers to ensure a wider coverage of the jamming.

The German equivalent of our A.I. was known as *Lichtenstein*, or *Li* for short, and it was just as susceptible to jamming as their other gadgets. Again this was dealt with by jamming aircraft flying with our bombers. Our boffins also produced 'Serrate', a device which actually homed on to the transmissions of the German *Li*. 141 Squadron, with whom I had done my first tour, had gone into 100 Group some months before 157 Squadron. They had been equipped with Serrate and had operated with remarkable success, homing on to German night fighters from as much as fifty miles.

Another device which helped to confuse the plotting system and the night fighters' *Li* was known as 'Window'. This consisted of strips of silvered paper which, when dropped from aircraft, produced false radar echoes. A small force of perhaps twenty bombers dropping, or rather scattering, Window would probably be plotted as two or three hundred aircraft by the enemy warning system.

The properties of Window had been known for some time by our boffins, but for security reasons it was not used by Bomber Command until the German night bombers were no longer a serious threat. The Germans did in fact use Window against Britain in early 1944, but by then Bomber Command had made extensive use of it to stimulate big raids and to create diversions which would often take large numbers of German night fighters away from our main bomber force.

With the advent of the German *Knickebein* navigation beam, a Radio Countermeasures Unit, known as 80 Wing, had been formed in 1940. From beam-bending it had concerned itself with jamming devices and such things, but it had been a ground unit. The various inventions were flown in aircraft of squadrons in all the groups in Bomber Command. It was decided later to withdraw most of the jamming aircraft from ordinary bomber squadrons and to bring them together into a new Group. This was 100 Group, The Radio Counter-measures Group, in which we were later to find ourselves with 157 Squadron. The job of 100 Group was to frustrate the German night defences, particularly their night fighters, which were by far the greatest menace to our bombers.

Chapter X

BOMBER SUPPORT

A BOMBER force operating over enemy territory constantly cannot stand more than a small percentage of loss to enemy action. To this loss must be added the inevitable losses due to training and flying accidents and to bad weather. The German day bombing of Britain had to be called off when losses mounted too high, and some of the early Bomber Command night raids suffered almost equally disastrous losses.

The formation of 100 Group with its jamming aircraft was only one of the steps taken to bring these losses down to sizeable proportions. The vital importance of the most careful planning of raids was realised and soon a remarkable amount of brains and ingenuity went into this planning.

Help was also obtained from Fighter Command in the shape of the actual transfer of night-fighter squadrons. Just as the German bombers had been harried from take off until landing, so too could the German night fighters be harried. That had been the role of 141 Squadron with Serrate, and now we were to join in the job of harassing, which was now given the name of Bomber Support.

There were two main reasons why bombers could not be escorted at night by fighters. One was the considerable difference in the speeds of bombers and night fighters and the consequent difficulty in maintaining station. The second and more important reason was that the main object for a Bomber Support fighter must be to destroy the enemy night fighters before they come near the bomber stream and lose themselves in it. Even with Mark 10 A.I. it would be impossible to pick out a German night fighter from a mass of British bombers, who would probably be dropping Window. It was therefore necessary to throw a screen of fighters around the bombers' target and, indeed, if possible, around the whole bomber route over enemy territory.

This screen of fighters would operate at about the same height or slightly below the bombers' height, in order to intercept enemy night fighters climbing up on their way to attack the bombers. Patrol points for the Bomber Support fighters would be about forty miles or eight minutes' flying time from our main bomber stream, so that once A.I. contact was obtained on an aircraft by a Bomber Support fighter, the interception had to be brought to a swift conclusion. In other words, less than eight minutes must pass between the original contact, the chase, the visual, the identification and the destruction of the aircraft if it were hostile. Other squadrons of Bomber Support fighters would operate as low-level Intruders at known German night-fighter bases.

A night's operations by Bomber Support fighters was worked in three phases. For the first phase a wave of low-level fighters, equipped with Mark 10 A.I. and carrying a couple of bombs, would take off to patrol as many as possible of the enemy night-fighter airfields likely to be involved in the night's raids. These aircraft were briefed to arrive on patrol before Bomber Command's main raid was plotted by the enemy radar. It was important that they should be sufficiently widespread to give as little indication as possible of the whereabouts of the main raid. If practicable, more than one airfield might be covered by a fighter. Once on patrol, the fighter would look for signs of activity and attempt to prevent, or at least to discourage, enemy fighters from taking off by judicious use of bombs and cannons. If any did take off, the fighter would try to shoot them down.

The second phase was a wave of fighters with Mark 10 A.I. but no bombs. These fighters would fly low on the first part of their journey so that they should not be plotted by the enemy until the last moment before their entry into enemy territory. They would then climb to operational height, say fifteen thousand feet, and arrive on patrol at a pre-set time, usually at about the time when the enemy would probably obtain the first definite plots on our bombers. Their aim was to screen the bombers from any enemy fighters who had managed to become airborne.

These high-level patrols were usually continued until half an hour or so after bombing was finished, and it was most unlikely that an aircraft on a patrol of this nature would not have at least one or more chases. After a chase the fighter would return to the original patrol point until it was due to leave. There was generally a brightly burning target left by the bombers by which the fighter could position itself. Then the target area itself was usually worth investigating in order to catch any late-comers from the Luftwaffe and to screen the returning bombers. On the way back from patrol the high-level support fighters were allowed to investigate any enemy airfields they saw illuminated in order to catch enemy fighters attempting to land.

The third phase was another wave of low-level fighters, again equipped with Mark 10 and bombs. They relieved the first wave, patrolling the enemy fighter airfields at which enemy fighters were expected to land and making things difficult for them. Obviously every airfield could not be covered and quite a number of enemy fighters continued to plague our bombers, but many more were prevented from doing so.

The main idea behind all Bomber Support operations was really to worry the German night fighters. Although a very large number of enemy fighters were shot down through these operations, the chief blow was at the morale of the German night-fighter crews. Any German night-fighter crew who managed to get airborne while his airfield was being patrolled, then made his way through the high-level patrol and found the bombers, faced up to their gunners, made his way back again through the high-level patrol, then landed at an airfield patrolled by one of our low-level fighters, could certainly be said to have earned his night-flying supper and ersatz coffee. Particularly as all the jammable equipment he carried had probably been jammed most of the time. It is one thing to be a hunter; to be a hunted hunter is a very different matter.

It will be realised from this that a major raid by Bomber Command required very careful timing and planning. It was not just a matter of detailing a number of bombers to attack a German town but of ensuring that the bomber force should have the fullest protection at all times and that things should be made as difficult as possible for the German defences. While the bomber formations were assembling over England, the ground jamming stations would begin operating. At the same time the airborne jammers would be in position forming a complete jamming chain to the east, the south-east and the south. These chaps would often operate from dusk to dawn, keeping the German defences on the alert all the time.

The tactics employed by the bombers themselves provided almost endless ways of foxing the German defences. On a night when a big raid was intended on a particular target, a secondary target would probably be attacked and one or more spoof raids would be organised. These raids could be co-ordinated in time so that they would appear through the jamming on the German radar all at about the same time. They would be heading on widely diverging courses, with the smaller number of bombers on the diversionary raids dropping Window as hard as they could in order that all the raids should appear to be of equal strength. Thus, from the very beginning the enemy would have difficulty in knowing how best to deploy his fighters.

Clever variations in the timing of the diversionary raids and the main raid could produce many headaches for the German controllers. It must be remembered that even the raids on secondary targets carried quite a sting. There might well be thirty or more heavy bombers as well as the 100 Group aircraft manning the diversion, and the German controllers could not ignore these raids, even if they suspected that they were not the main attack. These diversionary raids were also supported by Bomber Support aircraft. This served a double purpose: it helped to give the impression that they were indeed major raids, and if enemy night fighters were sent there some of them would probably be destroyed by the Bomber Support fighters.

Spoof raids were laid on, often with outstanding success. The Luftwaffe suffered from shortage of aviation fuel and oils – particularly from the end of 1943 onwards. A large number of their aircraft were concerned only with the defence of the Reich, and until things became really desperate a threatened raid would provoke strong reaction from German night fighters. The more we could persuade the Luftwaffe to launch fighters into the air unnecessarily, the more of their precious oil and petrol was wasted.

There were various forms of spoof raids. The most usual was for as many training aircraft as possible to assemble over Norfolk and then set off over the North Sea, to simulate a major raid heading for Northern Germany. There might be as many as eighty aircraft involved, and all the jamming and the Bomber Support patrols would be laid on to help the simulation of a really massive raid. Just before reaching the enemy coast, but not before they had been well plotted by the German warning system, the training aircraft would turn back, having carried out a good navigational exercise.

On several occasions spoof raids of this sort brought a reaction of two or three hundred German night fighters and a considerable waste of fuel. Apart from this, some of them were shot down by Bomber Support fighters. After one or two of these spoof raids, Bomber Command would probably lay on a major raid on the very same route and catch the German controllers out.

Even when the weather was poor or when Bomber Command was having a night off, 100 Group would usually arrange some activity to keep the Luftwaffe employed. There were very few nights from the end of 1943 until the end of the War when 100 Group had no aircraft over the Reich.

There were also almost nightly Mosquito raids on Berlin to

harass the enemy, and finally the tactics employed by the main bomber force could usually be relied upon to cloud the issue for him even more. One of the simplest methods of foxing the enemy was for the bombers to fly on a course which would make it appear to the Germans that the target was a town in mid-Germany, such as Mannheim. After the raid had been well and truly plotted, the main force might turn sharply north and bomb one of the Ruhr towns, while some twenty aircraft, dropping Window madly, would carry on towards Mannheim to keep up the deception.

With all the many ways they had of misleading the German controllers, Bomber Command had no need to follow any pattern in planning their raids. The Germans therefore were almost always forced to treat all plotted raids with the greatest suspicion and were hardly ever able to make the best use of their night fighters.

This, then, was the prospect before us now that we found ourselves members of 100 Group. So far as I was concerned it was a pretty pleasing prospect. I had complete faith in my pilot, in the Mozzie and in Mark 10 A.I., and here I was, sitting in the front seat for the all-out offensive for which every Briton had been waiting and hoping. If I had felt fairly sure before that I was on one of the most interesting and thrilling jobs in the war, I was absolutely sure of it now. It was going to be the Battle of Germany – we would be playing away from home from now on.

We had been forbidden to fly over enemy territory or even near it with our new equipment until ordered to do so. When we received the order we knew that something special was afoot; it was on June 5th, the eve of D-Day. I had been doing some Mark 10 instructing in a Wellington in the morning. When I went to the mess for lunch I received the exciting news that we had been told to stand by for operations that night.

After lunch we did a night-flying test run in Mosquito 'E', which had been allocated to us and which was subsequently named 'Eager Beaver'. Eager Beaver became 'our' aircraft and we flew it whenever it was available for our Bomber Support patrols.

We were due to take off an hour before midnight. On this occasion we were not told much about the night's operations as an obvious security measure in case operation *Overlord*, the invasion of Europe, had to be postponed for any reason. All we knew was that Ben and I were to patrol Eindhoven airfield for forty minutes. Eindhoven was in southern Holland and was used as a German bomber base. All the patrol points for the two squadrons at Swanington that night were Intruder patrols on Luftwaffe bomber bases and all low-level patrols.

This was it.

All our experience and hours of practice was not to be put to the test. So often Ben and I had discussed our previous Intruder patrols and bewailed the fact that we had not been allowed to carry even the old types of A.I. with us. Now we were off on patrol with the most promising of all, Mark 10.

Anticlimax was to follow, however. We reached our target without incident; and although there was rather a lot of cloud we identified it clearly with the aid of a target map with which we had been provided. We could see the airfield runways, but no lights were visible, and we did not see any sign of activity at all during our patrol. Nor did we see anything else to shoot at on our way home although we looked jolly hard.

We had a similar patrol on June 8th, but this time we patrolled the neighbouring airfield of Gilze, as well as Eindhoven. We spent twenty minutes near each airfield, but, apart from arousing the curiosity of some searchlights who failed to illuminate us, we saw nothing of interest. Nor had anybody else from the two squadrons at Swanington so far.

The C.O. and one of the Flight Commanders of 157 Sqadron had been posted just before we began operations with 100 Group. On June 9th Wing Commander Ken Davison, D.F.C., arrived to take over the Squadron and Ben was made acting Flight Commander of 'A' Flight.

We were not required for operations for the next three nights, but Ben and I had a useful couple of hours on the night of the 11th chasing another of our Mozzies whose pilot had been briefed to give us some really difficult evasive action. We then acted as target for him and both crews found that Mark 10 was extremely good for chases of this sort, which we might expect in our new role.

The next night we were detailed for a low-level patrol of three airfields near Rheims: Laon/Athies; Laon/Couvron; and Juvincourt. We had been there on an Intruder patrol almost a year before but this time we had Mark 10 A.I. with us. Just before midnight we took off, climbing to five thousand feet on our way south; over the Thames Estuary, where they forgot to fire at us, then losing height on our way to Beachy Head, which we crossed at one thousand feet.

We were in Eager Beaver and she was flying perfectly as we continued losing height to cross the Channel at two hundred feet. As usual, just before we were due to reach the French coast we climbed to three thousand feet and made a good land-fall at Criel, near Dieppe. As we set course for our patrol area, Ben remarked:

'It's a blooming dark night, chum. I reckon it would be as well to stay up here. We certainly won't see much if we go down.'

'Suits me,' I replied – and it did too.

We were much more likely to pick out pinpoints to help my navigation from three thousand feet than if we had gone lower. Then, even with Mark 10, I would get better results with the extra bit of height. Laon/Couvron was reached at 01.15 hours. Nothing was stirring there so we began the rounds of the three airfields.

What with watching A.I., keeping my log up to date, taking an occasional Gee fix and peeping out for landmarks, I was kept fairly busy for the next twenty minutes. Then I heard Ben say:

'Hullo. Hullo. Hullo. What's going on there?'

I looked up and saw that a cone of three searchlights had appeared some eight or nine miles ahead of us. It seemed to be about halfway between Juvincourt and Laon/Couvron. Ben had already opened up the throttles and we were heading for it.

'This might be it,' said Ben. 'Keep your eyes skinned. Any joy yet?'

'Not a sausage, I'm afraid. Blimey O'Reilly! Wouldn't it be lovely if there were something there. Are the searchlights still on?'

'Yes. They're on all right. Keep your ruddy head in that box.'

The seconds ticked by. Then, after about two minutes with Eager Beaver fairly whistling along:

'Contact!' I yelled. 'It's well above; range three miles. Turn starboard.'

'Turning starboard. How far above?'

'Thirty degrees. Keep turning starboard, range still three miles. He's way above us. Keep climbing.'

'Turning starboard and climbing.'

We soon found that our quarry was orbiting the cone of searchlights. By turning harder, we cut down the range and Ben got a visual of him silhouetted against the searchlight beams, just over a mile away now but still well above. Whatever it was, the aircraft was too far off for Ben to identify it. We found to our dismay that it was outclimbing us. We had got up to nine thousand feet by now and the range had started to go out again.

Ben gave Eager Beaver all the urging he could, but gradually as we tried to climb up after it the range increased. Now it was nearly five miles away. We had been chasing it for twelve minutes. It was infuriating.

Suddenly my heart leapt. Another blip had appeared on my A.I.

'Turn to port. I've got another contact. Range four miles, it's crossing from starboard to port, only slightly above.'

'Thank the Lord for that. Turning port. What's happened to the other one?'

'It's gone altogether now. Ease the turn . . . steady. Range three miles. It's very slightly above.'

'Steady. Leave it a bit above. How are we doing?'

'Fine. This one seems to be flying straight and level. We're coming in a bit too fast. Throttle back.'

'Throttling back. What's the range?'

'Just two miles . . . coming in very nicely. Where will you want him?'

'Keep him above and a bit to starboard . . . about ten degrees I should say. What's the range?'

'Gently port . . . about four thousand feet now. Still coming in nicely . . . steady now. He's ten degrees starboard, slightly above . . . Range just under three thousand. Throttle back now.'

'Throttling back . . . Range?'

'Just about two thousand. He's still ten degrees starboard five degrees above. Any luck?'

A few seconds' pause that seemed like hours – then:

'A-a-a-ah! I think I can see him. Hang on to the contact. I'll go in a bit.'

'Okay. Good show!'

A few more seconds passed. I could see the blip coming in to eight hundred feet. Then came the words I was waiting for.

'Okay, have a look now. It's a Jerry all right. Looks like a Junkers 188.'

I looked up, my night vision needing a few seconds to adjust itself. I saw a dark shape which gradually resolved itself into a Junkers 188. We were almost directly underneath it, just about four hundred feet below. Ben eased back the throttles gently, lifted Eager Beaver's nose slightly and at a hundred and fifty yards' range fired a three-second burst at the Junkers.

There were strikes on the starboard wing roots and the starboard engine caught fire. A further two-second burst blew pieces off the port wing tip. A short third burst produced strikes on the burning starboard engine. Then the whole of the port wing outboard of the engine broke off and passed under us. A second later the Junkers hurtled straight down in flames and exploded on the ground.

I had been entering up my log and then took a Gee fix which showed us to be over the Forest of Compiègne. It had taken just under four minutes from obtaining contact on this second air-craft to seeing it hit the ground. From the light of the burning starboard engine we had seen a swastika on the tail and dark green camouflage on the upper surface of the wing.

The time for the finish of our patrol had been up some minutes so we set course for the base, which was reached without further incident. We landed just after three a.m. and everyone was highly delighted that the score at Swanington had been opened for 157 Squadron. For our part, it was certainly satisfying to have had an early success with Mark 10 on this new job. As for our ground crew, they had painted a swastika on Eager Beaver almost before we were out of the cockpit.

Once the ice had been broken, more successes followed quickly for the Squadron. A Junkers 88 was shot down the very next night near to where we had found our victim. The night after this, one of our crews, Flight Lieutenant Matthews and Flight Sergeant Penrose, shot down a Junkers 88 and damaged another near Dieppe.

Ben and I carried out three more low-level Intruder patrols in June, visiting airfields in Belgium, France, Holland and Germany. On the first occasion we were patrolling an airfield near Lille while our bombers were raiding Lens and Valenciennes within a few miles of us. We had a grandstand view of the bombing, which was very impressive, but we saw nothing else of interest. The two other patrols were also without incident.

Chapter XI

THINGS THAT GO BUMP IN THE NIGHT

On June 27th Ben and I were not on the programme for that night. Patrols had been allocated to the crews who were flying, and take-off time for all of them was around midnight. Suddenly word went round that all Bomber Support operations by 157 Squadron aircraft were cancelled and all crews were to report to the briefing-room immediately for a special briefing. And a special briefing it certainly turned out to be. I know that as far as I was concerned I had the impression by the time it had finished that Jules Verne had come to life again and now held an important post at Air Ministry.

We were to be transferred, at least temporarily, to an operation with the code name of *Diver*. We were given all the available information about this new operation. Some small sort of aircraft which were to be regarded as Top Secret and which would be referred to as Divers, were expected to make attacks on the London area. It was rumoured, but not known, that these aircraft were pilotless. In the summer of 1944 this took some believing!

We were to assume as a safety precaution that they did carry a pilot. The actual size of the Diver was not known but it was believed to be slightly smaller than a single-seater aircraft. Large numbers of the Divers were expected and we were told that they would probably fly at about two thousand feet and at a speed of around three hundred and fifty miles an hour. This was too fast for a Mozzie to catch under normal conditions and

149

we were therefore to patrol at about nine thousand feet in order to be able to gain speed in a dive. Perhaps this was where the code name came from.

The Divers were expected to leave the French coast in the area of the Somme Estuary. They were thought to trail fairly long exhaust flames by which we should be able to spot them from some distance. We were to patrol the French coast in the expectation that we would be able to see these flames as moving lights. We were then to dive to intercept them and attempt to shoot them down into the Channel if possible.

Our patrol line was about twenty-five miles long. On one leg we were to fly north-east and on the return leg we were to fly south-west. Several other aircraft from A.D.G.B., Air Defence of Great Britain, as Fighter Command had recently become, would be on patrol with us. The patrols were arranged to cover the entire night. As so many aircraft would be involved, two simple precautions were to be observed. In order to obviate the chance of head-on collisions, aircraft on the north-easterly leg were to fly at odd thousands of feet – nine thousand feet if cloud conditions permitted, but if they did not, at seven thousand, five thousand or three thousand. The return leg was to be flown at even thousands of feet.

The second precaution was that as soon as a fighter turned to chase a Diver it must at once switch navigation lights on. These must be left on until the chase was completed. If any enemy night fighters showed up we were expected to look after ourselves, though Control would warn us if their presence was suspected.

It all seemed too utterly improbable to be true.

A maximum effort had been asked for. The normal method of arranging the operational programme each day was for Group to enquire what would be the maximum number of fighters that were certain to be available with crews from the station for the night's patrols. Depending on the importance of the night's operations by Bomber Command, Group would ask either for a maximum effort from the station or for some part of what they knew we could produce. If twenty aircraft were asked for, obviously ten from each squadron would be involved. Group would allocate ten patrol points to each squadron and the Squadron and Flight Commanders from the two squadrons would decide which individual crews would take each patrol point.

As Group had called for a maximum effort we made sure Eager Beaver was in fighting trim. She was and at 22.55 hours Ben and I found ourselves airborne on an anti-Diver patrol over the Somme Estuary. There was one small change to our usual set-up; the armourers had been instructed to load us with one tracer in every four of our cannon shells. Normally we did not use tracer ammunition in order to maintain the element of surprise. We were soon over the Channel making our way to our patrol point. When we reached it, we informed Control. The weather was clear but dark, so we turned on to our north-easterly leg flying at nine thousand feet.

'Well, here we go,' said Ben. 'Some caper this is. I wonder what bright spark at Air Ministry dreamed this one up?'

'Blowed if I know! I'm certainly going to keep my A.I. switched on. There are dozens of aircraft around.'

'Yes. The Jerries are bound to plot a gaggle of aircraft like this. If they put some fighters up there'll be some fun.'

'I should say so.' I took the visor off the A.I. indicator. 'Just look at this! There're five aircraft here for a start!'

'Not to worry,' he sighed. 'Press on regardless!'

We pressed on regardless for some forty minutes of our hour's patrol with our remarks getting more caustic all the time. France seemed very dark and peaceful below us. It all seemed such a waste of time. Then suddenly it happened. Down there in the blackness we saw a moving light. It was followed in a matter of seconds by another and another, until within a minute there were five little lights below all heading north-east for London.

Ben was already turning after the leading light. I switched the navigation lights on and stared out at the moving lights which were all heading in the same direction but with a considerable space between each of them. They were yellow.

I looked at the one we were diving after. It was some way

off still but we were fairly whistling down after it. All seemed to be well, then suddenly:

'Christ Almighty!' exploded Ben. 'Just look around us. Let's get to hell out of here!'

I looked around. The sky around us was stiff with navigation lights. Almost every fighter on patrol must have seen the lights at the same time and gone screaming down after the leader.

We weaved our way through the navigation lights. Ben wasted little time and merely transferred his attention to number three of the lights. This was about a mile behind the first one. Eager Beaver was shuddering a little as we were now diving at well over three hundred and twenty miles an hour – pretty fast for an ordinary night-fighter Mozzie.

Ben had judged the interception beautifully. The Diver was now fairly close below our starboard wing, crossing slightly from starboard to port. All that could be seen was a long yellow flame. What the devil could it be?

As Ben made the final turn to bring us behind the Diver, or whatever it might be, we lost sight of it for a second. Then a huge yellow flame swooshed just over our cockpit. We had found it again – the flame looked at least twenty feet long.

The Diver was whizzing along very fast indeed at a height of two thousand feet and flying straight and level. Ben had to keep the throttles full open to keep up with it although we had gathered quite a lot of speed during our dive. We were nicely behind it now.

'Here goes,' said Ben, giving the thing ahead of us a two-second burst of cannons.

The tracer shells in our ammunition proved their value. But to our dismay we could see them falling well short of the wretched flame thing in front of us.

'It must be a damned sight farther away than it ruddy well looks,' remarked Ben, giving it another short burst. 'It seems to be about two or three hundred yards.'

The shells were still dropping short. With each burst of fire our speed had dropped slightly. Even with full throttle Eager Beaver was falling behind. Then a thought struck me. I had

152

been sitting there feeling a bit useless on this job, but as Ben was finding difficulty in judging the range, I could give him the correct range from my A.I. Sure enough I could see it clearly, only a small blip but easy to see. I told Ben:

'I've got it on A.I. The range is nearly six thousand feet.'

'Well I'm blowed! I would have thought it was still only about five hundred yards off. Well, it's no use chasing this one any more.'

As we climbed back to patrol height we discussed the strange phenomenon we had seen. It had flown straight and level even though we had been firing tracer at it. It all seemed very queer, but perhaps it might be a pilotless missile after all.

I was quite pleased that I could be of some help: using my A.I. as a range finder. We were over the Somme Estuary again, but we could see no more of the yellow lights. The patrol carried on for another ten minutes or so, then we saw another batch of five Divers start off on their journey. This time we had decided to ignore the leading light – which seemed far too popular. We swooped down after number three, with our navigation lights on as before. This time as I looked around I could see only one other pair of lights in pursuit of the Diver. Ben had spotted it too.

'Is he the only one around?' he asked.

'Can't see any more . . . No, nobody else near, anyhow.'

'Right, we're in a better position than he is. Flash the nav. lights on and off a couple of times and see if that works.'

I did as Ben suggested, but the other aircraft's navigation lights were still there – a little further behind but still there. I reported this to Ben. He was now approaching the tricky part of the whole business, the final swoop.

'Okay. We'll soon fix him.'

Although we were still some way from the Diver, far out of firing range, Ben let fly a short burst of cannons. We saw the tracer falling away in front of us. So did the other aircraft. He must have realised that we were better placed for an interception, so he waggled his wings and turned away. Just in time too – Ben did not want anything else to worry him now.

The Diver was down on our starboard side, coming in to us at an angle of about fifteen degrees. Ben had kept it below so that he would be able to swoop on it after the final turn that would bring us behind it. He timed it perfectly. As we turned, he put Eager Beaver's nose slightly down and I could see the blip on the A.I. The only information he wanted from me was the range.

'I've got it now. Just under a mile . . . we're closing on it nicely . . . three thousand. How's it going?'

'Oh, we've still got a bit of height in hand. It looks bloody close now. What range?'

'Two thousand . . . it's still coming in quite fast . . . fifteen hundred now . . . twelve hundred.'

'I'll have a go from about two hundred yards. Can't see anything to shoot at but that ruddy great flame. What range?'

'Just under a thousand feet. We're still gaining pretty fast.'

'Yes. This isn't going so fast as the first one was.'

'Coming in to eight hundred now . . . seven hundred, still gaining . . . coming in to six hundred.'

'Okay. Here we go.'

I looked up as Ben pressed the gun button. We saw the tracer go slap into the flame. Flashes came from it as the shells struck home and sent it spinning into the sea. The strange flame from its tail was still burning until it hit the water.

In the meantime, as Ben gave the fairly long burst of cannon fire, Eager Beaver bucked for a moment or two like a Wild West broncho. The cockpit was suddenly filled with cold, rushing air; there was a noise like a heavy sea breaking on a shingle beach and the wind whistled into the cockpit like a hurricane.

For the first and only time in all sorties together Ben said to me:

'You'd better put your parachute on, Brandy.'

So I did.

After a few moments, however, Eager Beaver seemed to settle herself down to fly fairly smoothly. Ben decided to make for the nearest airfield in case of emergency, as there was obviously something amiss. I gave him a course to steer for

Tangmere. I remember hoping that if we did have to jump for it we would at least reach dry land before the worst happened. I am a very keen swimmer, but I prefer to choose the time and place.

We reached Tangmere in due course, with Ben flying very gingerly. Eager Beaver seemed none the worse for this short trip, so we agreed to carry on to Swanington. It was always a bit of a bind to have to land away from home. Although visitors to an airfield were usually very well taken care of, we had no overnight kit with us and we did not know how long the repairs to the aircraft were likely to take.

As we approached Swanington Ben called Flying Control to let them know we were on our way. They wanted to know if we had had any luck. Ben said that we had got one and that our aircraft was damaged but he thought there would be no trouble in landing it. Nor was there any trouble. When we landed, two hours and forty minutes after take off, we were quite pleased and excited with our night's work. We were also pleased to be down in one piece, although I had not really been able to believe that Eager Beaver would let us down.

Quite a crowd was waiting to receive us and to find out what this Diver business was all about. We told all that we knew. Later we found out that only two Divers had been shot down that night and ours had been the first by about twenty minutes. I believe that we were in fact the first crew to shoot one down at night.

Next day the whole story of the Divers was released. They were the wretched things known generally as buzz-bombs to the public but as Divers or Beechcraft to the Services.

It was found that Eager Beaver's nose had almost collapsed with the excessive strain caused by our speed coupled with the vibration from the cannons. After this, the noses of Mozzies flying on this job were strengthened. We had certainly found the tracer ammunition useful, and the tip of using A.I. as a range finder was passed on.

We were told that we would be kept on operation *Diver* for

a while. Swift modifications were carried out to all the Mozzies. The exhaust shrouds were dispensed with, extra boost was given to the engines, we were supplied with 150 octane petrol and, of course, the noses were strengthened. With the exception of the exhaust shrouds, all these modifications were retained when we returned to our Bomber Support role.

We carried out a similar patrol two nights later but no bombs appeared while we were on our beat. The damage to Eager Beaver was not very serious, but it would take four or five days for the repairs to be completed.

July turned out to be a very eventful month. To the great joy of the whole squadron Ben was promoted to Squadron Leader and made 'A' Flight Commander. At about the same time I became Squadron Navigator Leader. This meant quite a bit of extra work and responsibility for us both, but Ben made a first-class Flight Commander, whilst for my part I liked having a say in the things that mattered.

On July 2nd we shot down another buzz-bomb while we were on a similar type of patrol as before. Again we found that four or five of them were launched together and we made straight for number three. We were the only fighter after it and we had no trouble with it. The next patrol, on July 5th, produced another buzz-bomb destroyed. On this occasion, however, the brute just would not go down until Ben gave it a really long burst of cannon fire. We were back in Eager Beaver and the vibration from the cannons put some of the instruments on Ben's blind-flying panel out of action. We landed at Ford for repairs at three in the morning and had to wait over two and a half hours before we took off again for Swanington, where we landed at 06.15 hours.

We were off again just after midnight for another anti-Diver patrol. We were lucky enough to shoot down two of the things on this trip. Again we went after the third of a group of four or five of them. We found nobody else after our first victim and only one other fighter after the second. Ben had the whole business so well taped by now, though, that he easily out-manoeuvred the other chap and we were soon in much the

156

better position to deal with the interception; the other chap saw this and cleared off.

Once the excitement of the first couple of patrols was over, it really was an unrewarding job for the navigator. He was responsible for navigating to and from the patrol line, but after that about all he had to do was to keep his eyes open for activity, let his pilot know the range when they were after a Diver and feed him with barley sugar or chewing gum from time to time. Our extensive training was being wasted.

The one weakness in the Bomber Support Mozzie in relation to its particular function was that Mark 10 A.I. searched only forwards. There was no warning if an enemy night fighter came up behind. Our Radar Section, under its very keen officer, Flying Officer Davies, had been working on a tail warning device which they had christened 'Monica'. On the night of July 10th it was fitted into two Mozzies. Ben and I went up in one of them with another crew in the second aircraft. Monica worked like a charm. It gave pretty reliable warning when the other aircraft came within six thousand feet of us and we were full of its praises when we landed.

Permission was sought from 100 Group to fit it in all 157 Squadron aircraft; not only was this granted, but Monica became standard equipment for all 100 Group night fighters.

Next day we had the bright idea of using Monica as an extra offensive weapon. We went up with another crew whom we had briefed about our idea which was to allow the other Mozzie to stalk us while I watched its range as it came in. I could read this off my Monica tube. When the range came down to between three thousand and four thousand feet, we whipped round in a tight turn which brought us nicely behind the stalking aircraft. It worked too.

Although I felt a slight sense of frustration at having been taken off the exhilarating job of Bomber Support to chase buzz-bombs, there was a special satisfaction for me in seeing the wretched things go down into the Channel. I knew that they were intended for London, and I was born in London.

One hundred Group must have appreciated how I felt. On

the 12th we were given a low-level support patrol, and two days later a high level one; both were uneventful, however. The 17th saw our last success against the buzz-bombs, making our score six in all. On this occasion we took off at the ungodly hour of 03.30 hours and found our bomb just as we were due to finish our patrol. In fact we did a few minutes' overtime.

We had found that in almost every instance Ben must have shot away part of the buzz-bomb, making it turn one way or another and plunge into the sea with its flame still alight. On one occasion only had the flame gone out and then it had just nosed straight down into the sea. We were very lucky in this respect, for it was such a small target that it was necessary to get to within two or three hundred yards to have a good shot at it.

The Divers were not always as amenable as we had found them. Flight-Lieutenant Matthews and Warrant Officer Penrose from our squadron had a rather shattering experience one night. They were on patrol and intercepted a Diver. Matthews opened fire a little too soon and had a rather long chase before he shot it down. Not long after, on the same patrol, they had a second chase. This time he was determined to go in close before he opened fire. He did. The thing exploded right in front of him. His Mozzie was thrown about like a feather in a storm for a few seconds. Then he realised that he could see nothing through his windscreen but a warm red glow was coming from behind him somewhere. His fin and rudder was ablaze but a few gentle dives blew that out. With the aid of his navigator he managed to wipe the windscreen clear of some of the soot and muck from the bomb's explosion. Very gingerly he flew the damaged Mosquito back to base, where he landed all right. He informed his ground crew that he thought there was a bit of damage at the back, which they had better look at next morning.

The whole station looked at it next morning – it really was a sight to behold. Only the framework of the fin and rudder was left, the rest had burned away. Every scrap of paint on the starboard side of the aircraft had been burnt off. The camouflage paint, the roundels and the squadron markings had completely disappeared; on the port side the paint was still there but it was blistered all over. They had certainly had a narrow escape. These two went on to become one of the highest scoring crews on 157 Squadron.

Towards the end of July it was decided to put both the Swanington squadrons on anti-Diver patrols full time. On the 21st the squadrons were transferred to West Malling in Kent, in order to be nearer the scene of operations. Although we were disappointed at being taken off our other job, there was some slight consolation in being moved to such a very pleasant part of the country in the summer. The 157 Squadron mess was at Addington House, a really lovely mansion set in delightful grounds. In these grounds were some of the most beautiful rose beds I have ever seen. They were tended by a sect known as the Seekers. Each rose tree was dedicated to the memory of some loved one who had died. I must say that the rose trees were much more pleasing to the eye than a cemetery full of tombstones.

Addington House was about four miles from West Malling and we used to travel past hop fields on our way to and fro.

Only Sussex and Cheshire can compete with the wonderful hostelries of Kent for dispensing the product of the hop. One of these hostelries, the Rose and Crown at Dunton Green, had been taken over just before the war by two very dear friends of mine from pre-war days, Mr and Mrs Byrne. We had many pleasant times with them during the next few weeks.

Nearby at Tonbridge there was a roadhouse, Hilden Manor, with an extremely nice swimming pool in which I had often swum. By dint of a little organisation we were soon carrying out dinghy-drill practice at Hilden Manor and we managed to arrange transport there on almost every fine day. It was a fine summer that year and we certainly made the most of it.

Ben and I flew on one more anti-Diver patrol from West Malling before going off on three weeks' leave. On July 23rd we took off at 03.30 hours and made for the usual patrol point near the Somme Estuary. This time there was a considerable amount of cloud down to about three thousand feet.

We would obviously have seen nothing if we had flown above the cloud, so we were forced to fly below it. This proved a double handicap. Not only did it mean that we would not be able to gather speed in a dive, but our field of vision was sadly reduced. We saw three of the wretched things which we might have caught with a little more warning and a few knots more speed. As it was, we had three maddening chases with the buzz-bomb just out of range by the time we had got behind it. Although Eager Beaver was straining every nerve we just had to sit there and watch them draw away from us – really frustrating.

When Ben and I returned to West Malling after our leave we found a complete transformation in the anti-Diver set-up. By now the interception of these things had been brought to a fine art. One lot of night fighters chased them across the Channel to within about six miles of the South Coast, where the guns, heavy and light, took over from them to four miles inland. From there more night fighters, in which were included two squadrons, operated with the aid of searchlight boxes; these fighters took up the chase as far as the barrage balloons. Very few bombs were getting through now. In the beginning, the day and night fighters had shot down the greater number of the bombs. Now, with a greater concentration of guns combined with better warning and equipment, the guns took a heavier toll. Between the 14th and 26th of August Ben and I flew on four of these new patrols without one bomb coming into our patrol section.

It must have become obvious to the enemy that, as his launching sites were being overrun by our invading armies, he would have to find some other way of launching the buzz-bombs. Their answer was to fit them beneath aircraft which had begun operating from bases in southern Holland. These aircraft would fly out towards our East Coast at very low altitudes to avoid detection by our long-range warning system. They would then pop up to about two thousand feet to launch their missiles and then head back home.

On August 18th we were sent on a low-level patrol just off

the Dutch Islands. The idea was to try to intercept the launching aircraft which were mostly Heinkels. If we could shoot the Heinkel down before it launched its toy, so much the better.

Almost from the moment we arrived on patrol we began a series of chases that got us nowhere. We spotted some lights on one of the islands, but they went out as we approached and we could see nothing when we got there. Then we had two long and difficult chases on aircraft, both of which turned out to be Mosquitos. We then saw what we thought must be a launching some way off. No A.I. contact appeared, however. Again we saw a launching some distance from us but had no joy when we investigated it. Finally we returned to West Malling tired and rather dejected.

At last came the day we were all waiting for. On August 27th we were taken off Diver operations and returned to Swanington.

Divers, buzz-bombs, Vee-1s, Beechcraft or flying bombs, call them what you will, they were certainly a most ingenious weapon. I do not believe that they constituted a war-winning weapon, but properly used against the south of England when the invasion forces were being assembled, they might well have changed the course of the war. It is difficult to imagine how it would have been possible to build up the vast quantity of invasion material if it had been subjected to constant bombardment by buzz-bombs. It was originally intended to send over several hundreds a day beginning in January 1944. One can imagine the chaos that would have been caused on the South Coast.

The bombing of Peenemunde and the constant attacks on launching sites had helped to delay the initial launchings until July. Even then, Hitler regarded the 'V' weapons purely as a retaliatory measure against London. In spite of great pressure, he would not allow them to be used elsewhere until it was too late. It must be remembered that it took almost three months for the defences to finally win the battle against the buzz-bomb. Even then, it was largely due to the fact that many of the

161

main launching sites had been overrun by the advancing Allied Armies.

I have often been asked if it was true that pilots had actually destroyed buzz-bombs by formating on them and tipping them over. This did happen – only in daylight, of course – but it was essential that the aircraft performing this dangerous feat was faster than the bomb. Tempests and the latest Mark of Spitfires came into this category, and so, later, did the Meteor.

Chapter XII

A BEAM IN YOUR EYE

WHILE operation *Diver* had been in progress, 157 Squadron and our stable companions, 85 Squadron, had done their best to keep a strict training programme going in readiness for the return to Bomber Support. When we returned to Swanington, however, we found that we were to be given a week to get back into full swing again.

One of the first things we did was to arrange to hold an Extraordinary General Mess Meeting to discuss ways and means of providing ourselves with a decent bar for the mess. We had previously made do with a small dispensary for drinks. Now, having seen the many very pleasant drinkeries down south, we were all very discontented with our lot. Ben was elected President of a Bar Committee, and in a very short space of time a really delightful bar had been constructed entirely on a self-help basis. A large and unlikely looking cellar was transformed into an attractive and comfortable lounge bar, and the squadrons were to spend many an enjoyable evening there.

Another big improvement that we found on our return was in the Operations Briefing Room, which had been organised and was run by the Intelligence Section. It was a very important part of the station set-up and had been treated accordingly. In a spacious room were chairs and tables on which the navigators could spread out their maps to plot the night's operation. The walls of the room had been covered with some boarding in which pins could be easily inserted, and almost the whole of one wall was covered with maps which had been assembled to cover practically the whole of Europe.

Every scrap of information pertaining to our job was available to us for the asking and the scope of this information was a constant source of amazement to me. Our first briefing in the new room was on September 5th when the two squadrons were first put back on to Bomber Support operations. It was most impressive and became the standard method of briefing while we remained at Swanington. The entire night's operation by Bomber Command was depicted on the huge wall map. Coloured tapes were pinned to the map showing the route to be followed by Main Force bombers; white tape denoted the route to the target and black the return route; diversionary raids – that is, secondary and spoof raids – were also shown with tapes, usually of red and blue.

Our patrol points were indicated by flat-headed pins with the numbers 85 or 157 on them. Group would allocate them to the squadrons en bloc and the Squadron and Flight Commanders would assemble before briefing to sort out each patrol separately for the individual crews. German fighter assembly beacons were shown by black-headed pins. All sorts of other relevant information was available – the disposition of searchlight and flak belts, for example – and all was presented in a manner easy to digest.

The patrols called for on September 5th were in support of a spoof raid on Hanover. The weather was pretty poor here and Main Force bombers were not operating. A combined force of 100 Group aircraft and Pathfinders from 5 Group were going off in an attempt to get German night fighters airborne and make them waste fuel. High-level support aircraft were operating with them to help simulate a major raid and to chase any Germans who might be up.

A small target-marking force of Pathfinders would make for Hanover, where they would drop their marker bombs and some incendiaries. They would be followed by some twenty heavy aircraft from 100 Group, dropping Window. Meanwhile the support fighters would have taken up positions around the route and target areas.

This part of the briefing was done by the Station Commander or one of the Squadron Commanders. It was followed by a talk by the Intelligence Officer, who would pass on any extra information he had been able to ferret out. Then Signals and Armaments Officers would have their say. Finally the Met Department reported on weather and gave us forecasts of wind strengths and directions at various heights.

Once briefing had finished, there would be a hubbub of voices as each crew sorted out the details of their own particular trip. No two would be the same, and all we were normally given as far as our own instructions were concerned were the patrol point, the time we were to arrive there and the time we were to leave the patrol area.

The spoof raid on Hanover was carried out as planned. The only thing that went wrong was that the Huns refused to co-operate. This time they remained steadfast on the ground and not one of our fighters had a chase. Probably the weather over Britain was so bad that the Jerries knew that Bomber Command would not put on a major raid. Whatever the reason, we saw nothing on our high-level patrol just to the south of Hanover.

When our patrol time was up, we decided to go down and have a look at Vechta, a German night-fighter station in the vicinity. Here, too, there was no sign of life. We then decided that, as it was very dark and hazy, there was little future in looking around much more and so we headed north, the shortest way out of enemy territory. We passed halfway between Emden and Wilhelmshaven, flying at three thousand feet, and then climbed to four thousand to dive over the coast at the little island of Baltrum, near Nordenery.

Nobody had taken any notice of us on our hour and a half patrol. We were clear of Baltrum and still on a northerly course; I was just saying to Ben:

'We can turn for home in a minute. Course . . . two-six-zero degrees. I think we're far enough out now.'

Suddenly two searchlights flicked out of the darkness straight on to us. One from Baltrum, the other from the mainland.

'Well, they've left that a trifle late,' I remarked.

'Have they indeed,' said Ben, stuffing Eager Beaver's nose down in a dive. 'They're firing heavy flak along those ruddy beams.'

So they were.

Luckily the flak was not as accurate as the searchlights. It was quite some distance behind us and soon gave up. The searchlights flicked out too; we were on our own again.

'Now that was an unsportsmanlike thing to do,' said Ben. 'You just can't trust those Jerries!'

We turned then and set off on the long sea leg back to base.

On the afternoon of September 11th we had carried out our night-flying test in Eager Beaver and had put in a good session of practice with Monica, our rearward warning device. We landed and decided to amble over to the Intelligence Section to see what was on for the night before going up to the mess for a meal.

On the way round the perimeter track Ben remarked:

'I think we'll let the other chaps have first pick of the patrols tonight. We'll take the one that's left over.'

I understood the reason behind this decision. Ben was always conscious of the ill-feeling that could build up on a squadron or a flight when the Commander invariably picked the most likely looking patrol for himself; or if on a defensive night-fighter squadron, he stayed on the ground when things were quiet but leapt into the air whenever Huns were around. That might have been a good way of building up a big individual score, but it was by no means the best way of building up squadron morale.

One of Ben's jobs as Flight Commander was to allocate the various patrols to the crews in his Flight who were on operations on any particular night. He was very much aware of his responsibility in this direction. He would certainly never shirk a patrol that looked difficult, but at the same time he realised that because morale was so high on the squadron all the crews wanted a really fair chance of excitement and action.

166

I must say, though, that when we saw the operational plan for that particular night it looked as if we could not have picked on a worse night for such a decision. A gigantic raid had been laid on for some poor unfortunate town in southern Germany, with a secondary target in the Ruhr. With one exception, every patrol from Swanington was in support of one or other of these raids. They looked just the thing to provoke massive reaction from the German night fighters.

There was just one solitary patrol that was not in direct support of these two raids. It could not, in fact, have been much further away from the main scene of activity; it was right up on the island of Seeland, just off south-eastern Denmark, and it was off all the maps and charts we normally used, as it was so far to the north-east.

There were no other patrols of any sort anywhere near it, but a spoof raid that looked rather ineffectual had been laid on. Some training aircraft were scheduled to pop out over the North Sea and to fly towards northern Holland before turning back for home. It did not look to us as if the spoof could possibly have any real bearing on our patrol point, which was miles away.

We had realised at once that we would be left with this stooge patrol as we were taking last pick. Sure enough that was how it turned out. There was just a little consolation for us when we learned from Intelligence that there was a German fighter beacon on Seeland. This was one of the fighter assembly beacons which normally consisted of a light on the ground that could be seen from some considerable distance flashing a letter in Morse code to identify it to the German night-fighters. There was, as well, a powerful R/T transmitter which would be tied up with the reporting system and would pump out information to any German fighters who might be ordered to assemble there.

However, this beacon did not seem much consolation for what would be a round trip of over a thousand miles, with a twenty-minute patrol thrown in. We noted that we would have to pass fairly near to the airfield of Westerland/Sylt, so we determined to have a look there on the way back if, as we were pretty sure, the Seeland patrol turned out to be a waste of time.

We had a leisurely meal in the mess, accompanied by a few sarcastic remarks about our apparent night off ops. Then we went back for final briefing and at 20.45 hours carrying what seemed to be an excessive number of maps and plotting charts, we climbed into Eager Beaver. As we taxied round the perimeter track to the end of the runway, I could not help feeling a little peeved that Ben should have chosen this night of all nights to make this gesture. Anyhow, here we were and I might as well make the best of it. We were at the end of the runway now. Ben ran up the engines in turn, with the brakes hard on, checking his instruments. I glanced round the cockpit to check that oxygen was on and everything else all right, looked at my watch and as we started off down the runway, entered the first item on my log sheet.

I felt the usual thrill of excitement as we took off into the night. There was something about it that never failed to give me a kick, even on a stooge trip such as this. We were a minute or so early, so we circled the airfield twice before I told Ben to set course. The night was dark, with no moon, but there were no clouds either, making visibility quite good. We made height to two thousand feet and crossed out over the Norfolk coast just south of Cromer. Our long sea leg of over four hundred and fifty miles had begun.

Eager Beaver's twin Rolls-Royce Merlin engines were purring smoothly. I switched on the A.I. just to check if it appeared to work all right; it did. I switched it off as we did not want to be plotted by the enemy radar. A transmission from our A.I. would be picked up much further away than they would be able to see the aircraft. We had dropped to about five hundred feet, which also gave them less chance of picking us up.

All we could see was sea and stars. The seemingly endless sea journey soon became monotonous. We were the only moving thing except for an occasional falling star. The sea beneath us was horribly black. I took a Gee fix. We were pretty well on track; the forecast winds had been good so far. Nearly two hours had gone by before we reached our patrol point. I passed Ben some barley sugar and had some myself. I always took a selection of things to suck on these patrols; we were issued with quite a choice – fruit drops, barley sugar, Horlicks tablets or chewing-gum. One's mouth got very dry sometimes, and it gave one something to do.

There was quite a bit of German jamming on Gee now, but I got another good fix. We could not expect to pick it up much longer at this height, anyhow. We had decided to steer fairly well clear of Sylt, our landfall would be at a little island just north of the island of Sylt. Five minutes before we were due at the island I told Ben. There was a slight change in the note of Eager Beaver's engines as we began to climb up to four thousand feet. Soon we could pick out our little island just over to starboard. We could see the northern tip of Sylt as we turned slightly to starboard for the leg to Seeland.

We had decided to carry out our patrol at twelve thousand feet. It seemed as good a height as any so we continued on our way, climbing steadily. We were over the mainland now, no lights below and nothing to see on my A.I. which I had switched on as we started climbing. Monica was on as well and nothing showed on that either. Soon we had another short sea trip to cross and, in spite of the darkness below, we could see the coastline coming up.

We crossed the strip of sea and were halfway over the next piece of land when, far ahead, we spotted a flashing light. It was flashing the letter 'Q' in Morse.

At least the beacon on Seeland was working. After flying for another ten minutes or so we passed right over the beacon, and as we did so we saw the lights of neutral Sweden a few miles to the north-east of us. It seemed very strange to think that over there lived a nation not at war. However, we had our own little war to get on with, so we turned south-east on to our pre-determined patrol line. A four-minute leg that way, then about turn and an eight-minute leg the other way; that was the plan.

Once we had remarked on the proximity of Sweden there was nothing much to talk about. Nobody was taking any notice of our presence so far as we knew. We reached the south-east point of our patrol, and as Ben began the wide sweep that would bring us back on to our new course I gave him some chewing gum and bemoaned the fact that we had no cards with which to while away the time.

We had hardly settled down on course when I noticed with surprised excitement a faint blip on my A.I.

'Contact,' I yelled.

'Don't be funny,' said Ben disgustedly.

'I'm not kidding! Range nearly eight miles . . . coming in a bit bloody fast! It's a head-on just out to port. Get ready for a hard starboard turn. Range six miles.'

'Okay. I wonder what the devil this can be?'

'Range four miles . . . Still out to port and slightly below.'

'Do you want me to go down?'

'No. It must be on a parallel course, range three miles . . . Ready for the turn . . . Now!'

I know that as the turn starts I will lose the contact as the other aircraft goes out of our A.I. coverage. I also know that I should see it again very soon, crossing us from port to starboard. If I have judged the turn right, he should finish up about two thousand five hundred feet in front of us. It went very well. Fifty seconds later:

'Okay. I've got him again. Range three thousand . . . Gently starboard . . . Go down.'

'Gently starboard, going down.'

'He's turning starboard . . . keep going starboard . . . harder starboard . . . level out now but keep going starboard . . . range coming in a bit now just over two thousand.'

'We're going round the ruddy beacon. He must be orbiting the thing. Where is he now?'

'Two thousand . . . Keep going starboard . . . Ease the turn a bit. Where do you want him?'

'Starboard will do. Is he above us?'

'Just a shade . . . Coming in to fifteen hundred, still going starboard. He's about ten degrees starboard slightly above.'

'We're still going round the beacon . . . Ah! There he is.'

'Can you hold him? What is it?'

'Can't see what it is. Yes, I've got it all right now. It's bloody dark though; I'll go in a bit. It must be a Hun. What the hell would one of our aircraft be doing here?'

By this time we were underneath the aircraft only about four hundred feet away. It certainly was dark, but we could clearly see that it was a Junkers 188.

It had stopped turning starboard now and was flying straight and level. He obviously did not imagine that there was a Mosquito underneath him. Ben eased up Eager Beaver's nose as we dropped back slightly. As the Junkers drifted into his gunsight he gave it a four-second burst. The cannons rattled, the familiar smell of cordite wafted up. We saw strikes as flashes came from the starboard wing root. The Junkers gave a great lurch and lost much of its speed; Ben had to pull up over it to avoid a collision. As we went up over it, a four-star cartridge, two red and two green, was fired from it. By the light of these we saw the enemy aircraft drop very steeply away to starboard. A pinpoint of flame from its starboard engine spluttered into a large flame that we watched going earthwards.

Although I had watched all this from my grandstand seat with much excitement and gratification, my training ensured that I kept half an eye on Monica and half an eye on my A.I. In the same second that the Junkers started on its way down I noticed another blip on my A.I. It was about five miles ahead of us, slightly to port and a little below.

Ben needed no urging to believe me this time. As we turned after this second aircraft, we saw the first one crash on land just about three miles east of the beacon. It could be seen burning there for some time.

Meanwhile we were closing in nicely on number two. We decided that it must be an aircraft carrying out some sort of exercise with the first one. It seemed incredible to us that he had not seen all the commotion going on behind him. To our amazement, however, we had no difficulty in closing in on

171

him quite quickly. We repeated the tactics as before and identified him from close below as another Junkers 188 flying straight and level.

What a clot he must have been.

A four-star cartridge had been fired and an aircraft had gone down in flames – in fact it was still burning down below – and this chap had not noticed a thing.

As Ben lifted Eager Beaver's nose once more, I said:

'Make this one a real flamer.'

'Okay,' replied Ben, 'I'll see what I can do!'

This was not just bloodthirstiness on my part; we carried a ciné-camera which worked automatically with the cannons. At night it needed something pretty spectacular to register anything at all.

Ben proceeded to carry out instructions. He gave it a two-second burst from only a hundred yards. It straightaway caught fire in the fuselage, pulled up to port, then over the vertical in an almost classic loop. It dropped flaming like a torch to hit the sea only a few miles off the coast of Sweden with a magnificent flash as it exploded.

Some fairly large chunks had come off his Junkers as the cannon shells ripped into it. We flew right through them, but apart from feeling his slipstream and getting a horrible whiff of ersatz German oil in the cockpit, we suffered no damage – at least, not as far as we could tell.

These two one-sided contests had occupied just over seven minutes, so that we had only three more minutes left of our patrol time. In view of the fact that we had flown through debris from the second aircraft, we decided to call it a day. We still had a long sea journey to negotiate and it would be silly to take any unnecessary chances.

We set course for home. As we passed over the beacon it was still busily flashing the letter 'Q'. I had a momentary thrill when I saw something on my A.I., but whatever it was the blips were too blurred to be aircraft blips. We decided that it might have been Window that had been dropped earlier by the aircraft we had chased; we carried on with the return journey.

The excitement was not quite over, however. We were just crossing out to the north of Sylt when I got a contact on Monica. I saw it first at about six thousand feet range, warned Ben and when it came in to just under four thousand feet we whipped round in a hard turn to see if we could turn it into an A.I. contact.

We did not succeed in getting A.I. contact, but we shook off the aircraft that had been behind us. As we were still at ten thousand feet, Ben put Eager Beaver's nose down slightly so that we could gain a bit of speed on the way home. With all the night's thrills behind us the long sea journey did not seem too bad. We landed at Swanington after four and a half hours of what had turned out to be a very satisfactory stooge patrol.

The Mozzies from the other patrols had all landed by the time we arrived. Strange to say, only one of the 157 Squadron aircraft that had been on patrol that night had a chase and that resulted in one Junkers 188 damaged.

We found next day that apart from being covered in ersatz oil Eager Beaver had only a few scratches from the debris of the second Junkers. Later we were told that the film from the camera gun had shown evidence of the combats. I must admit that I was pleased about this. To return from a patrol that looked as pointless as ours had done and then claim two enemy aircraft destroyed seemed almost too much to believe.

Chapter XIII

TEAM-WORK

ONE of the most important jobs on a night-fighter squadron was the crewing up of pilot and navigator. It was one of my responsibilities, in conjunction with the individuals concerned and the Flight Commanders, to advise and make suggestions as to the best way of ensuring that a happy 'marriage' ensued on all occasions. In most cases the crews had been paired originally at the Operational Training Unit. Usually these pairings had been made after careful consideration and it was only rarely that changes were needed. The job we were now engaged on demanded keenness and initiative equally from the pilot and the navigator. A brilliant pilot could expect little success if he was flying with a navigator who could not get the best out of A.I. or whose navigation was weak. The same held true for a first-class navigator with a poor pilot.

Sometimes re-crewings became necessary through illness or the occasional posting of one crew member to a job on which he could not be accompanied by his partner. The more experienced aircrew often needed very careful handling; having gained their experience and worked out their own methods with one partner, they might dislike the idea of starting again with another.

Flight Lieutenant Doleman, known to all and sundry as 'Dolly,' was a pilot on 'A' Flight who had somehow contrived to remain on operational flying practically throughout the war without being sent for a rest. He had been crewed with a series of navigators in the past, but something always seemed to happen to them and he had never settled down with one for any length of time. In spite of numerous night patrols Dolly had not enjoyed any success, yet I felt sure he was a pilot with above average ability. I had flown with him on one or two occasions and I also knew that Ben had a high regard for him.

I have never come across anyone keener on flying and the Royal Air Force than Dolly, who really seemed to live for flying. He had two other loves: an ancient Rover car named Roger and a delightful smooth-haired fox terrier named Towser. Towser was a great favourite with us all and became the squadron mascot. As for Roger, with the help of some rope to keep the doors on and plywood to keep the wind and rain out where the side windows had broken, he went on forever.

Once an even older Roger made an appearance on the station; Dolly had bought it for spares. It was obvious to everybody that the older Roger was in much better shape than the real Roger. We wondered what Dolly would do. It would have been much easier to strip the real Roger for spare parts and ride around in Roger the Second. Dolly's love was too great, however; he retained Roger the First and for weeks the ghastly skeleton of Roger the Second lay near 'A' Flight dispersal until Dolly was ordered to remove it forthwith.

Operational aircrew were given generous and fairly frequent leave, but Dolly could only rarely be persuaded to take leave at all. Even then, on more than one occasion he had to be literally ordered off the station by the Squadron Commander.

Shortly after I became Navigator Leader, Dolly's navigator had been taken off flying for some reason or other. They had not been together very long but they were getting on well and at last it had looked as if Dolly was fixed up. Losing this last partner had made Dolly extremely brassed off and he confided as much one night in the bar to Ben. Next morning in the Flight Office Ben brought the subject up.

'I'm a bit worried about Dolly,' he said. 'He seems to be having more than his share of bad luck with navigators. In fact he's so brassed off that he has almost given up the idea of

175

ever getting a Hun. He was telling me last night that as he doesn't seem to be able to crew up with a navigator who is any good in the air, he may as well pick a good boozing partner! Evidently there's a chap at one of the O.T.U.s just due to come back to a squadron. He knew him some while back and wants us to try to get him here. Dolly's a good man, it seems wrong to me. What do you think about it?'

I had already thought about it. I had asked Group for a good replacement for the navigator who had gone, but there just was nobody available then. On 'B' Flight there was Flight Lieutenant Bunch. He was an experienced navigator and had been flying with the Flight Commander, whose place had been taken by Ben. 'Bunny' Bunch had already won the D.F.C., and, as he was slightly senior to me, he had undoubtedly been disappointed when I was made Navigator Leader. To be fair, he did not ever show any resentment to me and always proved helpful and co-operative. He was awaiting a posting which would almost certainly have been as Navigator Leader on another squadron.

'What about Bunny Bunch?' I suggested to Ben. 'I did mention it to Bunny the other day. At least he could get a bit of flying in until his posting comes through, but he's got the idea that he and Dolly wouldn't hit it off.'

'It might work,' said Ben. 'Bunny's a bit of an old sobersides, but I should think it's worth a try.'

I buttonholed Bunny at the first opportunity. He was not going to be the difficult one to persuade, I felt. Sure enough, he agreed to give it a try – anyhow, as a temporary measure. But I must fix it with Dolly. He would not approach Dolly about it himself.

That was the first round won.

Dolly proved a bit more difficult. He gave me all the arguments he had given Ben the previous evening, but I have a knack of getting my own way. Eventually he said, grudgingly:

'All right, Brandy me boy. I'll do it for you, but, by Golly, I wouldn't have done it for anyone else.'

On September 12th off they went on their first patrol together. It was a high-level Bomber Support patrol in the Frankfurt area and they succeeded in destroying a Messerschmitt 110. In the six months that followed they remained together as a crew, destroying six more enemy aircraft and damaging another.

Both of them were married soon after the War. I wonder if Dolly still drives around in Roger, but I do not think it likely. Roger could not really be described as a woman's car.

Although normal day-to-day servicing of our Mozzies was carried out at the Flights by the ground crews, they were given regular overhauls which might take a week or so to complete. Eager Beaver had been taken in for one of these inspections, so that we had to take another aircraft on September 13th when we went off for a high-level patrol just south of Koblenz.

We had not been in the target area for more than a few minutes when I picked up an A.I. contact. For the next ten minutes or so we were led a really merry chase. The aircraft we were following took continuous violent evasive action. Hard turns in either direction would be interspersed with steep dives and climbs, so that we felt rather like a yo-yo on the end of a string as we chased him. It took an age to reduce the range but we gradually closed in.

The evasive action had been so continuous that we thought we were perhaps after another Mozzie who was seeing us on Monica. If not, it might possibly be a German night fighter with a tail-warner. Eventually our quarry eased off his evasive action a little, thinking perhaps that he had thrown us off when we were, in fact, close up to him.

We sat underneath him and identified him as a Junkers 88. Ben used his normal manoeuvre of easing up the nose of our Mozzie and dropping back to firing range. As he did so he exclaimed:

'Confound this bloody gunsight. I can't dim the wretched thing properly. Look, it's like a flaming neon sign.'

Sure enough, when I glanced over, I saw a bright-red ring showing on his gunsight. There was a knob to turn so that the pilot could choose the exact degree of brightness he wished for.

The dimmer had gone wrong, and every time Ben tried to take aim the silhouette of the Junkers disappeared in the bright-red light.

'Well! I'll have a go. If we sit here much longer he'll see us.' He pressed the gun button. 'Now what the hell's gone wrong? It sounds as if only one cannon is firing!'

We saw some strikes around the port engine. Instead of the usual healthy roar of the four cannons, however, there seemed to be only a measly pop-pop. It was a pity we were not in Eager Beaver!

The Junkers went down in a screaming dive and Ben lost sight of him. I could still follow him on A.I., though. We chased him from fifteen thousand feet right down to eight thousand feet, with some wild evasive action thrown in. Again he eased off after four or five minutes and we closed in once more. We could see sparks and flames coming from his port engine, but the propeller was still turning.

Ben gave it another burst, cursing the gunsight as he did so. The roar of the cannons was still sadly diminished, but we saw strikes along the fuselage. The Junkers then made a clever move. He seemed suddenly almost to stop dead; probably he had put down his air brakes. Ben had to pull up hard to port in order to avoid ramming him. Then down went the Junkers again in a steep dive heading for a bank of clouds. Although we whipped round after him and dived for the clouds we lost sight of him and also lost A.I. contact.

Next day we found that two cannons only had been working. On the night of September 15th Squadron Leader Chisholm, the 'B' Flight Commander, was posted 'missing' after a high-level patrol in the Kiel area. A rubber dinghy, similar to those we carried in the Mozzie, had been reported in a position on the sea which was near to Chisholm's route. Ben and I went out next morning with a couple of other Mozzies to search for him. We would not have been able to rescue him but we could have fixed his position for a rescue launch. Unfortunately, in spite of a long search, we were unable to find the dinghy.

Two nights later we went all the way to Schleswig/Jagel in

Jutland. This was not so very far south of where we had, our encounter with the two Junkers 188s. This time, however, we were not so fortunate. We patrolled for quite a while without seeing anything; then, five minutes before our patrol time was up, there was a cloud of blue smoke, a smell of burning rubber and my A.I. went phut. This turned out to be the beginning of quite a run of trouble with A.I., although we had been very fortunate with it so far.

This particular trip, however, had provided us with one of the most unforgettable sights imaginable. As we went out over the North Sea at dusk we could see literally hundreds of aircraft in the skies around us. The heavens were absolutely full, it seemed. Bomber Command had taken off in force for an early raid and we were overtaking them. At the same time, coming towards us were the Americans, who had been carrying out a big day raid. With their bombers were their fighter escorts, which made a truly impressive aerial armada.

Impressive as it was, it was becoming jolly dangerous as the twilight faded. I had switched on my A.I. to help avoid collisions, but the picture was so swamped with aircraft blips that it was impossible to pick a single aircraft out. I switched the A.I. off and switched on our navigation lights instead until things thinned out a bit.

Our next three patrols were all marred by A.I. troubles. On the first two occasions the failure did not occur until almost at the end of the patrols, which were uneventful. The third patrol was in an area south of Bonn on the night of September 29th. Cologne was being bombed and we had a grandstand view of the whole proceedings. The night was clear but dark, and visibility was extremely good. In the distance we could see concentrations of searchlights and the sparks which denoted flak as the bombers made their way in. At times the flak seemed to fill the sky. It seemed impossible that through all that fire some six hundred of our bombers were flying serenely on their way. If ever a job called for cool courage, that of the bomber crews did, flying night after night on heavily opposed raids such as this.

Soon the target markers went down, followed shortly afterwards by incendiaries. Then with the flak building up to a crescendo, the main bombing started. As the fires spread below and we saw the flashes of the bombs, the flak and the searchlights gradually died down but the bombing continued.

We had been patrolling while all this had been going on, but I had not picked up anything on A.I. About half our patrol time had gone when there was that blue smoke and dark brown smell as the A.I. packed up. We were useless up there without our 'eyes', so we decided to go home. We would investigate any airfields we saw lit up, just in case we saw an aircraft landing or taking off. We had been flying at fifteen thousand feet and began descending to ten thousand feet on our way home as it would be a better height under these circumstances.

We had not flown very far, however, when I noticed a contact on Monica, which was fortunately still working.

Normally we would have let him come in to four thousand or five thousand feet before turning in an attempt to get behind him and chase him with our A.I. This time, though, our A.I. was not working.

'Well,' said Ben, 'we can at least give him a run for his money.'

He began to take fairly strong evasive action. I watched the Monica indicator closely. The range increased slightly but the other aircraft was hanging on quite well. I informed Ben of this.

'Right,' was the response. 'He'll have to get pretty close on a night like this before he sees us. Let him get in to about three thousand feet, then I'll whip round and we might just be lucky enough to get a visual.'

I let the other aircraft come in as Ben suggested. We whipped round in no uncertain manner and both peered vainly into the darkness, hoping to see exhaust flames. It was no good, though, and so Ben flew straight and level for a while to give the other aircraft a chance of picking us up again. Sure enough it did. We tried exactly the same manoeuvre but again without success. After this we decided that acting as a decoy duck any more would be a waste of time. Ben put down the nose of our Mozzie and we headed for home without any more excitement.

My wife was expecting our first baby early in the New Year. She was living in Bath and I had a few days' leave to arrange for the confinement. This was accomplished satisfactorily, with everybody concerned being extremely co-operative at the sight of my R.A.F. uniform. While I was on leave I learned that Ben and I had both been awarded a Bar to our D.F.C.

Somebody in Public Relations must have handed out some information to the London Press. The *Evening News* ran a startling headline across the whole top of one of the centre pages:

Mr Chips the Second Shoots Down Six Flying Bombs.

while the *Evening Standard* proclaimed:

Double D.F.C. for Donat's Double.

All this was accompanied by photographs, stories and quotes from the official citation and certainly brought about a deal of leg-pulling when I returned from leave on October 10th.

We carried out half a dozen more patrols during the next fortnight without having a single chase on an enemy aircraft. That is not to say that we had no chases at all, we did in fact have several. The unfortunate thing was that every one was on a friendly aircraft. We spent many minutes sitting right underneath Lancasters, wondering what they would say if they had known there was a night fighter underneath them. The problem of identification on a really dark night was always difficult, for we realised that if a Lancaster saw a twin-engined aircraft approach him at night over enemy territory he was perfectly entitled to shoot first and ask questions after. From our point of view, even with a Lancaster it was essential for us to get really close in order to identify it. Just for the record we were never fired upon by one of our four-engined bombers. Whether this was because of our careful approach or their remarkable night aircraft recognition is, I suppose debatable.

During these patrols, I completed my thousand hours' flying. Ben and I had a very pleasant trip on October 19th. It had been decided that the Swanington Squadrons should use the airfield of Juvincourt, near Rheims, as a forward base – mainly for refuelling – for some patrols planned for us in the Munich area later in the month. Juvincourt was, of course, in Allied hands by this time, and Rheims is nicely situated in the centre of the Champagne country. When it became necessary for someone to fly there to ensure that facilities would be made available for us, that fact did not escape our notice. We found ourselves among the crew of an Oxford that flew to this centre of the champagne industry on that morning.

We concluded our business at Juvincourt and managed to arrange transport to Rheims for the early afternoon. We were shown over one of the famous champagne establishments and acquired a few cases of the sparkling beverage. One of the directors of the firm spoke very fair English and we had an interesting chat with him.

He told us that the Germans had not damaged anything there as they were very keen to keep the champagne industry going. As for the French, they had by devious means managed to hide away almost all of their really fine vintage wines from the Germans.

Unfortunately there were five of us in the Oxford and we had had to promise so much bubbly to various high-ups that we only received three bottles apiece for our troubles. Very useful, however, to put by for the wetting of the head of my expected child.

Towards the end of the month we flew on what was to be the most uncomfortable and frightening patrol we ever had. The weather over England was frightful and the main Bomber Command force was not operating. Hundred Group sent over a small spoof raid and Ben and I were detailed for a high-level patrol between the North German ports of Emden and Wilhelmshaven.

We took off at 17.55 hours – a nice early trip, we thought. Almost as soon as we were off the ground we went slap into cloud. Although we climbed hopefully on our way across the North Sea, we did not manage to find the tops of the cloud. In fact we did not emerge from cloud until we were just over Swanington three and a half hours later. We just had to assume that our navigation was going more or less correctly. We had no means of checking our position by visual means, and Gee, our navigational aid, was soon very badly jammed.

In our efforts to get above the cloud we had climbed at one time to twenty-five thousand feet without success. We decided to return to fifteen thousand feet and arrived at what we fondly hoped was our patrol point at that height. The patrol between Emden and Wilhelmshaven took about seven minutes. As we turned somewhere near Wilhelmshaven for the return trip, the cloud in our vicinity began to light up occasionally. At first we thought it was lightning but suddenly our Mozzie gave a lurch which coincided with some very pretty light effects in the cloud. Perhaps it was flak and not lightning after all.

We felt rather like an Aunt Sally at a fairground. It was quite obvious that, with the weather so bad here, the gunners below would know very well that there would be no German aircraft flying. They would therefore be under no misapprehension about our identity. We would never know for certain if it was flak or lightning or both, but just in case Ben made things a little difficult for gunners by varying height and speed as we went not very gaily on our way.

We were down for forty minutes of this patrol and we decided to stick it out although there was no chance of seeing another aircraft in all that cloud, even if there had been one to see. All bad things come to an end and eventually we were able to call it a day and turn for home.

Eager Beaver had been out of commission for almost the whole of October, but on the 29th she was ready for us to take to Juvincourt for the patrol near Munich which was to take place as planned. We did our night-flying test in the morning and took off for Juvincourt at 15.30 hours. We had a meal and took off again after a Met briefing for our patrol. We were just circling the airfield before setting course for Munich when Ben exclaimed:

'Just look at that starboard engine.'

I looked. There I saw the tell-tale signs of oil dribbling back from the engine cowling over the nacelle of the starboard engine. We had an oil leak.

A hurried conference ensued. We obviously would be mad to attempt to go on to Munich, much as we had looked forward to doing so. The oil-pressure gauge was only slightly down on that engine, but we could see the stuff bubbling from the cowling. If we landed at Juvincourt we would not be able to carry out our patrol even if the fault was repaired almost immediately. The timing on these patrols had to be exact. If the fault took some time to repair, we might be stuck there for any length of time. The prospect of that did not appeal to us at all.

We decided to return to Swanington. If we did run into trouble with that engine, we had another one left and Mozzies had a wonderful single-engined performance. There were plenty of airfields at which we could land in emergency so we pressed on home, rather disappointed that such a likely looking trip should have petered out in such a manner.

There was another big raid on Cologne next night. Our patrol was an unusual one; we had been detailed to patrol the target area for half an hour but not to begin our patrol until ten minutes after the last bomber should have left. Visibility was quite good when we arrived although there was a fair amount of high cloud. Cologne was burning and we could see the lights of many fires showing through smoke that was drifting across the city.

We had hardly settled down on patrol when I got a contact. We closed in on a Lancaster which Ben saw silhouetted against the background formed by the smoke below. Ben had seen him quite clearly and had made the identification at nearly four thousand feet. We wondered why he was so far behind the others and decided to follow him for a while. We slid out starboard and let him draw away to five miles while I continued to watch him on A.I. We were quite a bit faster than the Lancaster, so Ben flew a weaving course behind him.

After about five minutes, as we were turning back towards him, a contact appeared well over to our port side and some three miles behind the Lancaster. Aha! we thought; this is a German night fighter stalking the bomber. So we closed in and found that it was on the same course as the Lancaster we were even surer. We had to get in to one thousand two hundred feet before Ben got a visual on the exhausts of another four-engined aircraft – what a disappointment.

Still, Ben thought there was something strange about those exhausts. They were nothing like the Lancaster's in colour or shape, so we went right in for a close look from about one hundred feet below. To our surprise it was a Liberator. What on earth was a Liberator doing over there?

It was quite unmistakable, however, so somewhat reluctantly we let it go. We wondered if it might be a captured one that the Germans were using, but in our position we had no choice but to break away, wishing that we could borrow a searchlight for a second or two to see if the Liberator had roundels or a swastika painted on her.

On November 1st we were detailed for a low-level patrol of Fritzlar airfield, near Kassel. The weather in the area was shocking when we arrived, with low cloud for miles around the patrol beat. We stooged around for a while in cloud, then, as we were obviously not of any use there, we climbed up to nearly twelve thousand feet before we were clear. It was quite pleasant up there with a little moonlight. Some way to the north-west we could see a large hole in the clouds, so we went over to investigate.

There was a very big area free of cloud there, and as we dived down we could see that visibility was exceptionally good. We soon confirmed our whereabouts – Kassel was some three or four miles behind us as we continued our descent to three thousand feet. Almost at once we spotted a train, which Ben attacked with very good results. There were several strikes on the engine which emitted clouds of steam.

As we zoomed up from this attack we saw another train farther along the line. Ben dealt with this train as with the previous one. Soon after this the cloud closed in again so we climbed up once more and headed for home.

Chapter XIV

EAGER BEAVER'S LAST PATROL

WE flew our last patrol in Eager Beaver on November 6th. She was getting rather long in the tooth for this very testing job and the squadron was getting some new Mozzies. Koblenz was the target that night. As there were several German fighter beacons in the vicinity, we expected some action. Almost as soon as we arrived on patrol we got a contact. A long chase after an aircraft which was taking the most violent evasive action ended when our A.I. went dead just as the other aircraft seemed to have settled down on to a steady course.

Four nights later we were on a high-level patrol in the same area. Just before we reached our patrol point I had a contact on an aircraft coming towards us. For the next twenty-five minutes we were engaged in the most amazing night dog-fight without ever managing to get close enough for Ben to see what we were chasing. I followed him on A.I. through the most violent evasive action I had ever known. It seemed probable that he was either a Mosquito or a German night fighter equipped with a tail warner. Twice we went in really tight complete circles, which made it appear as if he was trying to get on to our tail.

Eventually he went down in a very steep dive which we followed to two thousand feet height before we lost him. Whatever it was, the pilot was extremely skilful. Luckily he met his match in Ben, otherwise we would have become the quarry.

We climbed back on patrol, disappointed but exhilarated.

Still, perhaps that one deserved to get away.

Hardly had we reached patrol height again than we had another contact. A visual took only four minutes this t me. The other aircraft was dodging around a bit but was flying rather slowly. Our airspeed was only a hundred and ninety knots. Although Ben got a quick visual, identification proved rather more difficult. We were underneath him looking directly up for quite a while before deciding that it was a Junkers 88. It was a very black night and there was a certain resemblance to a Mosquito. To make absolutely sure, Ben slid out first to one side, then to the other to see it from as many angles as possible.

Once we had assured ourselves that it was indeed a Junkers Ben went through the usual drill of dropping back as he lifted the nose of our Mozzie and gave it a one-and-a-half-second burst – exactly a hundred rounds of ammunition we found later. The result was spectacular. There was a very bright flash from the tail of the Junkers and chunks of debris rattled over the Mozzie. Down went the enemy aircraft almost vertically. We followed rather more gently. Although we lost sight of it, for it was not on fire, I was able to see it on my A.I.

As I watched the blip, I saw two smaller blips break away from the main one. I whipped the visor off the indicator unit of the A.I. and showed Ben this phenomenon. What we could see were probably two parachutes opening up as the crew abandoned ship. We orbited the area and a few seconds later we saw a big flash on the ground in a position just west of Mainz. This was over a hundred and twenty miles south-west of where we had picked up our original contact.

At midnight on the 15th we were off to the same area once more. We had the maddening experience of chasing five separate contacts each one of which finished up with a visual on a Lancaster. These contacts were well separated in time and position and were all obtained some time after the bomber stream should have been well on the way home. The final visual was on a Lancaster with one propeller stopped. As our patrol time was up by then, we decided to give this chap an escort to the Dutch coast. We therefore dropped back from him and I watched him on my A.I. screen to make sure that no German night fighter approached him. Ben had to weave from side to side so that we would not overtake him.

Not one of these friends could have had the slightest suspicion we were near them. As I have said before, any of our bombers were perfectly entitled to fire at a twin-engined aircraft that approached them at night without waiting to identify it. After all, the fighter would be using A.I., or rather *Lichtenstein* if it was a Hun. With this help it would come in from the darkest quarter; it would be armed with cannons; and if the bomber waited for the other chap to make the first move it would be too late. We were prepared for this, and although we intercepted over thirty of our bombers during our 100 Group patrols, we were never fired on.

The reason I am making this point is that when I came off operations in the February of 1945 I was sent on a lecture tour of stations belonging to 6 Group, Royal Canadian Air Force bomber group and to the Group Headquarters. My instructions were to put them completely in the picture of the various operations carried out by 100 Group to help the bombers, particularly from the night-fighter aspect.

I gave a series of lectures, usually to three hundred or more aircrew at a time. Invariably all the senior officers were there and the chaps made wonderful audiences, really attentive and interested in what I was saying. In the question period that followed each talk it became quite clear, however, that none of them believed that a Mozzie could approach them over enemy territory and sit below them as we had so often done. They agreed that they would fire on sight at any twin-engined aircraft under those conditions.

Perhaps it was as well that they had such faith in their warning devices. Anyhow, I soon caught on to the fact that it would be silly to press the point. I encountered the greatest disbelief of all, however, when I gave my lecture at the Group Headquarters.

During the first half of December we flew on half a dozen patrols. Bomber Command was roaming far afield over the

Reich now, so our patrols moved with them. We rarely had a trip of under four and a half hours, rather a long time for two chaps to spend together in the confined space of a Mozzie cockpit, and yet another reason why it was so important for a crew to get on well together.

At about this time we heard from Intelligence that the German night fighters had a new tail warning device which they called *Naxos*. We had suspected this for some time, but the Swanington squadrons were still managing to shoot quite a few down.

Another interesting story from Intelligence demonstrated that the German radio countermeasures chaps had been a little too clever on one occasion at least. When Mozzies equipped with Mark 10 A.I. had at last been allowed over enemy territory, the casualties amongst the German night fighters had gone up enormously – so much so, that the German boffins could not believe that it was entirely due to the A.I. we were carrying.

It so happened that just at that time a new I.F.F., Identification Friend or Foe, had been introduced into their night fighters. Immediately they jumped to the conclusion that we had somehow learned of this I.F.F. and were equipped with a device which homed us on to it. Orders went out to scrap the I.F.F. – which for all I know might have been wonderful – but, of course, their night-fighter losses did not go down.

On the night of December 17th Bomber Command's targets were Munich, Ulm and Duisberg. Munich and Ulm were way down in southern Germany and Duisberg just east of the Ruhr. Our patrol was in support of the southern raid and we were to patrol between Stuttgart and Ulm. We had not chased a Hun for over a month and were hoping our luck would change.

It was a long way to go, two solid hours each way for only a twenty-minute patrol. We wasted no time and made straight for our patrol point, crossing in over the Belgian-Dutch border and plodding on over land at fifteen thousand feet until we reached our destination. For twenty minutes we scoured the skies between Stuttgart and Ulm without anything appearing on our A.I., although we saw lots of activity where the bombing was taking place. We tried flying at ten thousand feet and eighteen thousand feet, but there was just nothing doing for us.

We had plenty of petrol left so we decided to go out of our way a bit and see what we might find in the Frankfurt-Koblenz area. This proved a happy decision. As we approached Frankfurt at about twelve thousand feet I got contact on an aircraft flying south. It was well above us so we whipped around and climbed after it.

Whatever it was, it was certainly flying fast and high. Try as we could, we just could not catch it. Eventually, when we were up to nearly twenty thousand feet, we lost him, still well above us and going like a bat out of hell.

It seemed as if this was just not our night.

Round we turned, heading for Frankfurt again, when we spotted a cone of searchlights shining up into the sky near Wiesbaden. We made for these, and a minute later I had another contact. Our combat report read as follows:

Squadron Leader Benson reports:

Contact obtained near a cone of five steady searchlights. Our height 16,000 feet. We followed down to 6,000 feet and up again to 12,000 feet. Target weaving violently and making steep turns in either direction. Then followed down to 2,500 feet still on A.I. and we found ourselves on the circuit of a fully lit airfield. Visual obtained on Junkers 88g, indicated air speed 320 m.p.h. height 2,500 feet. At this time we were certainly not more than fifty yards away and below the enemy aircraft. I raised the Mosquito's nose and was about to open fire (despite the fact that I thought we were much too close,) when we were illuminated by a searchlight. At this moment the Junkers 88 fired a four-star cartridge – two reds, two whites. These completely blinded me. As I knew we were dead behind him, I opened fire but saw no strikes. Then I saw the enemy aircraft, illuminated by the falling cartridge, below and peeling off to port. I jammed the nose down and had a quick shot which produced several strikes outboard the starboard engine. He continued steeply down to port and we followed him round to the other side of the airfield, going very fast.

We were again illuminated, this time by two searchlights. The enemy aircraft fired another cartridge which illuminated it and it was seen above us and slightly behind. Our height was then only 800 feet. We could not get into firing position and contact was lost. Several white cartridges were fired from the airfield, which we continued to patrol for some time afterwards without obtaining contact again. Excellent work by Flight Lieutenant Brandon, who kept contact despite violent and continuous evasive action of every sort, especially when below 2,500 feet. The dog-fight on A.I. before the visual lasted for nearly forty minutes.

Claim: 1 Junkers 88g damaged.

By this time Ben was truly a master of his craft. His instinctive reactions under extremely difficult conditions enabled him to get a good shot at the enemy aircraft when most pilots would have been completely put off by the searchlight at so low a height.

It was very bad luck that after we had such a long chase, the searchlight and the four-star cartridge should almost have blinded Ben at the very moment he was about to fire. It takes quite a time to regain one's night vision under such circumstances, yet he handled the Mozzie perfectly.

On December 23rd there was a spoof raid on Limburg, just north-west of our happy hunting ground of Frankfurt. We were airborne at the nice early hour of 16.45 for a patrol near Frankfurt. Soon after reaching our patrol point we had a chase which resulted in a visual on a Lancaster. Disappointed, we flew towards Wiesbaden where we found another contact almost at once.

We were at fourteen thousand feet. Our target was flying in a southerly direction and climbing, but at an incredibly low speed. Ben had to weave from side to side in order not to overshoot although we were climbing after it and the Mozzie was not too fast a climber. We followed the aircraft over the target indicators that had been dropped on Limburg. It then turned right about on a course that took it, and us, first over Wiesbaden and then south-west towards Neunkirchen. A chase of about half an hour.

During this time it alternated between the very slow climb up to eighteen thousand feet, level flight with violent weaves for a few minutes, then a rapid dive down to six thousand feet and the fantastically slow climb again.

Eventually Ben managed to get a visual and immediate identification on a Junkers 88. It was down at six thousand feet at this time and was flying level but weaving violently. Ben followed it through a couple of weaves and then gave it a short burst from two hundred yards. We saw no strikes. Although it was very dark we could still see the Junkers weaving from side to side. Ben followed it through three or four more weaves and then had a shot at it when it turned in towards us from starboard.

There was a large flash from the starboard engine. The Junkers dived steeply to starboard and we followed it down to a thousand feet before losing the contact.

We climbed to five thousand feet and circled the position for a while. Some three minutes or so later we saw a red flash below us to the south. This was followed by a glow which we could see through thin cloud. We could not be sure if this was from the aircraft we had attacked however. When we landed back at Swanington we claimed a Junkers 88 Damaged but next day Group raised the claim to a Probable as no other combat had been reported in that area around that time.

The next night was Christmas Eve. Bomber Command was to drop some presents on Cologne and Bonn. In the mess at Swanington it had been decided some time before to have our Christmas dinner on Christmas Eve. As a maximum effort had been asked for from the station for the night's operations, we were very pleased that we all had an early time for take-off. It was arranged that dinner would be held back until we returned, giving us something to look forward to.

We left Swanington at 16.30 hours on our way to Limburg. We had put in quite a lot of flying time in that area during the past few weeks and considered ourselves rather as specialists around Frankfurt – a couple of Frankfurters almost.

We had been on patrol at fourteen thousand feet for about half an hour when we obtained a contact. We were just north of Limburg and the aircraft was well below us. Down we went pretty smartly to eight thousand feet after a target that was flying level at that height but weaving quite violently. As we closed in, Ben had fleeting visuals two or three times. Each time, however, he could not hold on to them nor could he identify the aircraft.

We continued to follow him on A.I., and he turned through two complete orbits before settling down on a north-westerly course. Shortly afterwards we saw some target indicators go down ahead of us. We had closed in on the aircraft and Ben got a visual on a Messerschmitt 110 at a range of two thousand feet, silhouetted against the light of the target indicators.

'Okay. I can see him all right now,' said Ben. 'Just look at that. No wonder we've taken such a while to close in.'

As I looked up, I saw the Messerschmitt go across us from starboard to port. It went a fair way out to port, then went right up on one wing and came back in front of us, crossing the other way in this violent weave. Ben followed it through several of these weaves, fairly well throttled back and far more gently than the Messerschmitt. Then, from about a hundred and fifty yards he gave it two short sharp bursts, firing at the exhaust flames.

The second burst set the port engine and the whole of the port side of the fuselage alight. We dived under some large pieces of debris that came flying back and heard them swoosh above the cockpit. The Messerschmitt was well alight now and going down over to our starboard. We saw it hit the ground and explode near a small town by the name of Dottesfeld, where we could see it burning brightly.

'About bloody time we shot one down again,' remarked Ben.

'Look at it burning. I wonder if the camera gun would pick that up?'

'Why not have a go?' I suggested.

So we did.

We had a good look around to see that there was no high ground and Ben did two runs right down to within a few hundred feet of the burning aircraft. All in vain though, nothing appeared on the film when it was developed.

We landed back at Swanington at five minutes to nine. Dinner had been laid on for half-past so after a pretty rapid de-briefing we set off for the mess. We were fortified with the news that, in addition to our Messerschmitt, Jimmy Matthews and Penrose had destroyed a Junkers 88 and Dolly Doleman had destroyed two more Messerschmitts.

As can be imagined, this gave the squadron something to celebrate. Four enemy aircraft destroyed in one night was by no means a record, but this had been accomplished on Christmas Eve, just before a party.

A single crew from 85 Squadron had, in fact, destroyed four enemy aircraft in one incredible patrol over Germany on November 4th, 1944. 85 Squadron were our stable companions at Swanington and the successful crew was Squadron Leader Burbridge, one of the Flight Commanders, and Flight Lieutenant Skelton, the Navigator Leader. This crew became easily the top-scoring pair on the Bomber Support job.

At about this time there was an incident on 157 Squadron that might have had most unfortunate results. One of our rather inexperienced crews returned from a patrol one night and claimed to have destroyed a Junkers 88. They had shot it down somewhere near the Battle Area, which was then in Holland. We were all extremely pleased with this success, for of course there was no better way of gaining experience than by shooting down an enemy aircraft in combat. Our pleasure at this success was rather dimmed by the fact that on that night we lost one of our crews, their Mozzie having failed to return.

A couple of days later, however, we were overjoyed to receive a signal from Holland to the effect that both pilot and navigator were safe and would be back with us shortly. When they did arrive back it was revealed that, without a shadow of a doubt, our inexperienced crew had been the cause of their worries. It was not a Junkers 88 that the new boys had shot down, but one of our own Mosquitos.

The crew who had returned from Holland reported that they had been returning from a high-level patrol, during which their A.I. and Monica had both packed up. They were just approaching the battle line and the pilot was pointing out to the navigator the flashes on the ground ahead of them. Suddenly they heard a terrific bang. Immediately their starboard engine burst into flames. The pilot realised that they were being attacked by a night fighter, but he could do nothing about it, for the Mozzie was at once almost out of control. The port wing kept dipping down and he was finding that it was all he could do to hold the aircraft level.

He warned the navigator that they would have to jump for it, then told him to jump. When he attempted to get out himself, however, he found it extremely difficult. The small door through which he had to escape was on the starboard side. Each time he let go of the control column, the Mozzie dropped its port wing and he just could not get out of the door. Eventually, after a superhuman effort, he managed to heave his way out and parachuted down to safety.

I say, parachuted down to safety, but in fact, as he and his navigator floated down, the same thought was running through their heads. Which side of the battle line would they land on?

They both recalled having seen the line ahead, but had they passed over it before they were attacked?

Because the pilot had baled out some several seconds after his navigator, they had lost touch with each other. However, they decided independently to avoid capture if they were on the enemy side of the line. They remembered their escape drill, hid their parachutes and then holed up. After several hours they were both relieved to hear British voices and came out of hiding.

All their information tied up only too well with the combat

report made out by the Mozzie crew who thought they had destroyed the Junkers 88. Time, place, height and method of attack all corresponded exactly. There was no doubt about it and Group had to be informed that the claim of one Junkers 88 should be erased from the record.

I believe that no action was taken against the offending crew apart from an interview with the Squadron Commander and having to stand their victims a few pints of beer at the bar. There was little need for further action – they were far too horrified by their mistake.

This problem of night identification was always a tricky one. A fairly successful device, involving the use of infra-red lights, was evolved by our boffins late in the war. Nevertheless, if an aircraft being chased did not show identification, it still was not proof positive that it was a hostile aircraft. If the aircraft did show this identification, however, it would often save the fighter a long and unnecessary chase.

München-Gladbach and Bonn were the targets for Bomber Command on the night of December 28th. We went off again on a high-level patrol south-east of the Ruhr. We were airborne for over four and a half hours, but my log book says: *Uneventful patrol.*

Uneventful patrol: I suppose that is quite correct so far as the log book is concerned. In actual fact, every patrol was prospectively a thrilling adventure. We were pitting our wits and our skill against enemy night fighters who were similarly equipped to us. Furthermore, they were operating over their own territory with the aid of ground control – although the fact that our Mosquitos and A.I. were both superior to anything the Germans produced made up for that advantage.

The morale of the German night figher crews was very high when the fighters of 100 Group came into the picture. They had chalked up enormous numbers of successes against our bombers and had suffered very little losses in so doing. The almost immediate and considerable jump in the number of casualties to the German night fighters came as a severe jolt to them. Soon their mounting losses and the harassing tactics of the Intruder squadrons of 100 Group began seriously to affect their morale. To the 100 Group activities must be added the probability that most of the German night-fighter crews must have suspected by then that Germany was losing the war.

On comparing notes with other crews both on 85 and 157 Squadrons we found ample evidence that many German night fighters were being shot down after chases that seemed to prove that they were making little or no effort to approach the target area, or to get anywhere near our bombers. Certainly in November and December of 1944 there had been over a dozen combats with enemy night fighters who were flying aimlessly about when intercepted. They would often be weaving violently around but keeping well away from any obvious activity such as a burning German town.

For some while almost all German aircraft production had been devoted to the manufacture of fighter aircraft and a large proportion of these were night fighters. There was quite a large force of enemy night fighters opposed to us at first. We had started with only four fighter squadrons in 100 Group, two for low-level patrols and two for high-level. In early November 1944 two more squadrons entered the Group. For the first few months after D-Day, therefore, a maximum effort from 100 Group could produce only about sixty fighters at a time when the Germans could probably muster two or three hundred.

From November onwards it was obvious that a number of German planes took off at night only because they were ordered to and were then worried only by the thought of getting down all in one piece again after a suitable interval. As they were not under close ground control, they could toddle off to some safe-looking area well away from all activity; fly around for a while, shoot off a few rounds of ammunition and land back for their night-flying suppers with a grand story of their adventures against the British bombers. It was unlucky for some of them that our fighters were so spread around that the safe area did not always turn out to be safe at all.

Late in December Ben and I were told that we would be coming off operations in the near future. Bomber Command was shortly to open its own school for Bomber Support training. Ben was to be the first Unit Commander and I was to be Chief Ground Instructor. No actual date was yet known but it would probably be early in the New Year. In the meantime we decided to get in a few more trips if possible.

On New Year's Day we went off on a high-level patrol near Bonn. The target for the main force was to be three Ruhr towns. Knowing that our tour of duty was coming to an end, we were perhaps even more anxious than usual for some activity so that we might end on a good note. We had three chases on friends, one of which led us far to the south. By the time we returned to Bonn the bombing was all over and our patrol time finished.

It was a beautiful night, so we decided to go down for a Ranger trip on our way home. There was a fair amount of moonlight so we had a good chance of seeing something to shoot at. Sure enough, about thirty miles north-west of Bonn we spotted a convoy of lorries moving along a road. Ben gave the leading lorry a long and very accurate burst of cannons. We saw several strikes and the lorry went right off the road into a ditch. As we pulled away we saw that two or three others had finished up in the ditch. We were already about half an hour late, so we did not go round again for another crack at them.

When we arrived at Swanington we had been up for nearly five and a half hours. We were the last Mozzie on the station to land. When we taxied round to our dispersal hut and clambered out of the cockpit there seemed to be rather more than the usual crowd to meet us. In the forefront of the crowd was the Squadron Intelligence Officer. He came dashing up to me and said:

'Well, Brandy, you've got one Confirmed today at least!'

It seemed a strange greeting. I wondered what on earth he was talking about. Then it struck me that possibly one of the aircraft we had recently claimed as Damaged or Probably Destroyed had been upgraded by Group to a Destroyed. Still, it seemed a funny time to tell me that.

I suppose I looked rather blank, for the I.O. took pity on me.

'Not to worry, lad,' he said. 'There was a telephone call for you which came through just after you had taken off. I took it for you. It was from Bath. You are the father of a daughter.'

This certainly was a complete surprise for me. I had telephoned my wife only the night before. She had said I was not to telephone again for at least a week as the baby was not due for another fortnight and she herself thought it would be longer. However, Susan Jane had decided to come into the world on New Year's Day and was not to be denied.

I managed to wangle a flight to Colerne, an airfield near Bath, and arranged to be picked up from there a couple of days later, when I had reassured myself that all was well.

Mother and baby were doing fine.

On January 5th, 1945, the main target was Hanover. Our patrol point was near Osnabruck, some miles to the west. Nothing much happened for a while, then we got a contact which we chased towards the target area. I could see that the aircraft we were after was dropping Window. It showed up quite clearly on my A.I. screen so that it was most probably a friendly aircraft. Anyway, it was miles off the bomber route, and as we had nothing better to do we decided to investigate.

We had just identified it as a Lancaster when I got another A.I. contact. We chased this to the south of Hanover, where the bombing was in full blast. About ten miles south of the city the aircraft we were after began to spiral down very quickly. Although we followed it, diving steeply after it, we lost the contact below us. We circled down at two thousand feet for a short time, but as we did not regain contact we climbed up towards Osnabruck again. We had reached Minden, halfway between Osnabruck and Hanover, when I obtained another contact coming towards us.

We were at a height of seven thousand feet by now and the target was above us. We whipped round at the appropriate moment and found that the aircraft was flying almost due east. He was going very fast and climbing on a straight course as he went up. Ben had our Mozzie absolutely flat out for most of the while and gradually we began to close the range.

199

The aircraft led us over the southern tip of the Hanover fires and we were pounding along, still climbing after him. At long last we reached his level and at once Ben had a visual on two pairs of brilliant yellow exhausts. The other aircraft was two thousand five hundred feet away and absolutely level with us, dead in front. Ben found that as soon as he went down slightly he lost sight of the exhausts. This brilliant yellow was something quite new to us and we felt sure it was a Hun.

We kept slowly drawing in. At a range of eight hundred feet Ben identified it as a Heinkel 219 by its twin fins and the dihedral of the tailplanes. I saw by our altimeter that we were at nineteen thousand feet. No wonder it had taken so long to catch the brute – the Mozzie was not a particularly fast climber.

At a range of two hundred yards Ben gave two fairly long bursts from dead astern. We saw strikes from both bursts along the fuselage and from the port engine. Some large pieces came back from the engine and we dived to avoid them. The Heinkel went down in a steep dive to starboard. We were able to follow it visually at first, for a great sheet of flame came from the port engine and some more pieces flew off.

After a few seconds the speed of the dive blew the flames out so we continued to follow it on A.I. right down to six thousand feet. Still turning in a wide orbit to starboard, we followed it up again to twelve thousand feet. Then it went down again in a very steep dive that we were unable to follow. We remained in the area and about a minute later we saw it crash and explode. It remained burning with occasional explosions of ammunition until we left the position. That proved to be our ration of excitement for the night and we made our way home soon afterwards.

Next day our posting came through. We were to report to Great Massingham, about twelve miles from King's Lynn, on January 21st. We were ordered to take a fortnight's leave before reporting so that we could do only one more patrol.

We took off for a patrol in our favourite area of Frankfurt. We had been flying for about twenty-five minutes when I noticed that the generator voltmeter was reading low, just as it had on our very first trip over enemy territory. We had to turn back. It seemed an awful anti-climax. It was only the second time we had ever had to make an early return and it had to be on our final patrol.

Strangely enough, the only time I ever felt rather jittery during all my operational flying was just before this very last trip. That night as I went to bed I remember well a profound feeling of relief that it was all over. Although I had found operational flying exhilarating rather than worrying, I must have been under quite severe nervous strain all the same. It was not until I actually knew for certain that I was being taken off operations that the reactions set in and it lasted for three or four days.

I had flown on eighty-two defensive and fifty-three offensive sorties since the summer of 1941.

The superiority of the 100 Group Mosquitos and their crews is borne out by figures. Although we were operating against radar-equipped German night fighters operating over their own territory, during the ten months 157 Squadron was in 100 Group they destroyed thirty-six enemy aircraft, with five probables and thirteen damaged. They were also responsible for the destruction of thirty-eight buzz-bombs. The squadron's losses were only seven aircraft and six crews.

Our friendly rivals at Swanington, 85 Squadron, had even better results. I am not sure of their final totals but over ninety aircraft were destroyed altogether by two Swanington squadrons.

It is interesting to hear the story from the enemy point of view. Wilhelm Johnen, a German night-fighter ace who finished the war as Commanding Officer of a night-fighter wing, comments on the 100 Group Mosquitos in his book *Duel Under the Stars*. One of his chapters is entitled 'Achtung! Mosquito!' and in it he writes:

Fast Mosquitos from the mainland were despatched to join the bomber stream and take over the task of air cover. The Mosquitos lived up to their name. They were the night fighter's greatest plague and wreaked havoc among the German crews. The radar equipment of this wooden aircraft surpassed anything that had previously been seen. It was technically so perfect that at a distance of five miles they could pick the German night fighters out of the bomber stream like currants out of a cake. . . . It was incredibly difficult to get a bomber in our sights for the Mosquitos sought us out and sped like rockets to the aid of the bomber. Not only had we the enemy in front of us but also in our backs. All this was a great strain on the German crews. The losses rose appallingly . . . The Mosquitos not only pursued us in the bomber stream but, as a result of their enormous fuel capacity and endurance, waited for us as we took off from our airfields. They attacked us throughout the whole operation and interfered with our landing. It was almost a daily occurrence that shortly before divisional ops several Mosquitos would fly over the airfields and shoot down the Messerschmitts as they took off.

My heart goes out to those poor harassed German night fighters.

Ben and I duly reported to Great Massingham. We had both been promoted; he was now a Wing Commander and I was Squadron Leader. We had a very interesting time forming our new command, 1692 Bomber Support Training Unit. As soon as we had it running reasonably well, I was detailed for a lecture tour of Number 6 (R.C.A.F.) Bomber Group, as I have said previously. On the day I returned from this tour we heard that we had both been awarded the D.S.O.

We called in at the Station Equipment section to enquire if they had any D.S.O. ribbon. No, they were sorry but they had none in stock. Should they order some for us?

We thought that might take quite a while and, as we had decided to go into King's Lynn that afternoon, it seemed more sensible to get the ribbon there.

In King's Lynn we found an establishment that proclaimed

itself to be a Military Tailor. We entered and a young lady came to serve us.

'Do you stock medal ribbons, please?' I asked.

'Certainly, sir,' replied the young lady, reaching for a fair-sized box which she opened for our inspection.

There was quite a pretty selection of medal ribbons in the box but no D.S.O. ribbon.

We explained that there was no D.S.O. ribbon in the box and tried to describe what it was like.

'A broad pinky-red band with a thinner blue border on either side.'

'Just a moment, sir. I'll go and ask.'

She returned after a short while.

'No, I'm afraid we haven't anything like that,' she said, then, pointing to the box:

'Wouldn't one of those do, sir?' she suggested.

EPILOGUE

Looking back, I am very proud to have served in the Royal Air Force. I find it hard to believe that anywhere, in any war, has there ever been anything to compare with the spirit, morale and comradeship that existed on an operational Royal Air Force squadron during the last war, from the Commanding Officer down to the lowliest airman on the squadron.

As regards the job I found myself doing, I would not have changed it for any other. It was just right. It required initiative, intelligence and level-headedness. It provided excitement and interest on every trip. We were treated as intelligent adults. All this, against the wonderful background of squadron life, made my wartime service extremely happy.

In all probability it was the last occasion when men could sally forth to do battle with the enemy's champions like the knights of old.

Around the time of Dunkirk, the war looked pretty hopeless for us. History tells us that we were saved by the 'few', during the Battle of Britain. A large part of the credit for that victory must go, however, to the boffins who produced the radar which gave the early warning and the control that ensured the best and most economical use to be made of the few pilots and aircraft then available.

Although the word Radar is of American origin, being derived from Radio Detection and Ranging, it should be pointed out that we British were far ahead of the Americans in its development. From Sir Robert Watson-Watt's very fine book *Three Steps to Victory* I should like to quote the following:

Nowhere in the world did there exist in 1940 any airborne radar: when Bowen went to America as a member of the Tizard Mission he found early ground radar, but no airborne radar. The first airborne radar to be installed in an American aircraft was a British Mark 4 A.I., and it was installed, in the U.S.A., by British personnel.

From the official history of the U.S. Army Air Forces in the Second World War again I quote:

All radar equipment and most of the radio equipment used by the Eighth Air Force during 1942 and well into 1943 was of British design and manufacture.

Surely a feather in the cap for our boffins!

So far as the air war was concerned, once the problem of day bombing against this country had been solved by the Battle of Britain, the night bombing by the Germans assumed greater importance. Once again radar came to our rescue in the forms of long-range warning, the Ground Control Interception stations and the little black boxes of A.I. that went into the night fighters.

Incidentally, A.I. was perhaps one of the best-kept secrets of the war. When one considers the great number of people involved in its manufacture, servicing and actual use, it is amazing how few outsiders knew anything at all about it.

The next big step in the air war was from defence to offence. Once the Americans mastered the art of daylight bombing and, in conjunction with the R.A.F., began round-the-clock bombing of Germany, the war was won. In the meantime, however, the Royal Navy had to keep the sea lanes open and the Army had to go in and consolidate, both vitally important jobs in the last war, although it is highly unlikely that either would be necessary in the event of another war.

I am convinced that the one German decision that had far reaching effects which have perhaps not been realised was the decision that all fighters would be retained for the direct defence of the Reich. This resulted in the failure of the Luftwaffe to use squadrons of Intruders over here when the bomber offensive was building up, and even more so when it was reaching its height in mid-1944. If your cities are being attacked by bombers, the bombers must be harassed on every inch of their journey – and at take-off and landing too. An aircraft is at its most vulnerable when taking off or landing and an aircraft shot down in sight of its home base is a great morale destroyer.

In spite of this, the Luftwaffe did not use Intruders from the early part of 1941 until a last-minute flurry in late 1944.

A second let-off was the failure to use buzz-bombs against southern England when the invasion forces were being assembled.

Radar and the 'few' saved us from losing the war; to whom should go the credit of final victory?

There is really only one possible answer. It was entirely a matter of teamwork, and in that team, not necessarily in the order of their importance, were the three Services, our Allies, the Boffins, the Commonwealth, the British public and the incredible stupidity shown at times by Herr Hitler and his advisers.

This formidable team was so very ably led by the only individual that I firmly believe was irreplaceable, Sir Winston Churchill. In the darkest days he provided the inspiration that welded the country into the unified force that was essential for the winning of a modern war.

The other leaders, the admirals, the generals and the air marshals, who emerged from the war with great reputations, just happened to be in the right place at the right time. I believe that there were always men who could have replaced them and have done just as well given equal opportunities. There was only one Churchill.

Finally, from my personal point of view, I must mention again the extreme good fortune which followed me throughout my operational service in the R.A.F. I must also congratulate myself on my service, my comrades and my job, none of which could have been bettered.

NEL BESTSELLERS

T009 696	GLORY ROAD	Robert Heinlein 40p
T011 844	DUNE	Frank Herbert 75p
W002 814	THE WORLDS OF FRANK HERBERT	Frank Herbert 30p
W002 911	SANTAROGA BARRIER	Frank Herbert 30p
W003 001	DRAGON IN THE SEA	Frank Herbert 30p

War

W002 921	WOLF PACK	William Hardy 30p
W002 484	THE FLEET THAT HAD TO DIE	Richard Hough 25p
W002 805	HUNTING OF FORCE Z	Richard Hough 30p
W002 632	THE BASTARD BRIGADE	Peter Leslie 25p
T006 999	KILLER CORPS	Peter Leslie 25p
W005 051	GÖRING	Manvell & Fraenkel 52½p
W005 065	HIMMLER	Manvell & Fraenkel 52½p
W002 423	STRIKE FROM THE SKY	Alexander McKee 30p
W002 831	NIGHT	Francis Pollini 40p
T010 074	THE GREEN BERET	Hilary St. George Saunders 40p
T010 066	THE RED BERET	Hilary St. George Saunders 40p

Western

T010 619	EDGE – THE LONER	George Gilman 25p
T010 600	EDGE – TEN THOUSAND DOLLARS AMERICAN	George Gilman 25p
T010 929	EDGE – APACHE DEATH	George Gilman 25p

General

T011 763	SEX MANNERS FOR MEN	Robert Chartham 30p
W002 531	SEX MANNERS FOR ADVANCED LOVERS	Robert Chartham 25p
W002 835	SEX AND THE OVER FORTIES	Robert Chartham 30p
T010 732	THE SENSUOUS COUPLE	Dr. C. 25p
P002 367	AN ABZ OF LOVE	Inge and Sten Hegeler 60p
P011 402	A HAPPIER SEX LIFE	Dr. Sha Kokken 70p
W002 584	SEX MANNERS FOR SINGLE GIRLS	Georges Valensin 25p
W002 592	THE FRENCH ART OF SEX MANNERS	Georges Valensin 25p
W002 726	THE POWER TO LOVE	E. W. Hirsch M.D. 47½p

Mad

S003 491	LIKE MAD	30p
S003 494	MAD IN ORBIT	30p
S003 520	THE BEDSIDE MAD	30p
S003 521	THE VOODOO MAD	30p
S003 657	MAD FOR BETTER OR VERSE	30p
S003 716	THE SELF MADE MAD	30p

--- --- --- --- --- --- --- --- --- --- --- --- ---

NEL P.O. BOX 11, FALMOUTH, CORNWALL

Please send cheque or postal order. Allow 6p per book to cover postage and packing.

Name..

Address ....

....

Title ....
(JUNE)